# More Alive Under The Shadow

## Following The Footsteps Of Simon Peter

## Forrest Chaffee

CSS Publishing Company, Inc., Lima, Ohio

MORE ALIVE UNDER THE SHADOW

Scripture quotations are from the New Revised Standard Version of the Bible, copyright
1989 by the Division of Christian Education of the National Council of the Churches of
Christ in the USA. Used by permission.

Some scripture quotations are from *The Harper Collins Study Bible*, New Revised Standard
Version (New York: HarperCollins, 1989, 1993). Used by permission.

**Library of Congress Cataloging-in-Publication Data**

Chaffee, Forrest, 1932-
    More alive under the shadow : following the footsteps of Simon Peter / Forrest Chaffee
        p. cm.
    Includes bibliographical references.
    ISBN 0-7880-2611-9 (perfect bound : alk. paper)
    1. Peter, the Apostle, Saint. I. Title.
    BS2515.C43 2009
    225.9'2—dc22

                                                                                    2008027843

For more information about CSS Publishing Company resources, visit our website at
www.csspub.com or email us at csr@csspub.com or call (800) 241-4056.

Cover design by Barbara Spencer
ISBN-13: 978-0-7880-2611-9
ISBN-10: 0-7880-2611-9                                                PRINTED IN USA

*This book is dedicated to a congregation located close to the campus of Gustavus Adolphus College in St. Peter, Minnesota, called First Lutheran Church, which has just celebrated its 150th anniversary.*

*It is a magnificent group of people who love their music and their singing reverberates with a deep and abiding faith. Among the people are professors, teachers, missionaries, retired pastors, and many others who love to study the holy scriptures.*

*The Monday Bible study classes were initial recipients of this study of Simon Peter. Their reflections and feedback have enriched beyond measure the great truths of this study. This book is also dedicated to them.*

# Table Of Contents

Foreword                                         7
    by Jerry L. Schmalenberger

Prologue                                          9

Forgiveness Under The Shadow                    13
    *Matthew 26:69-75*
    *Mark 14:66-72*
    *Luke 22:54-62*
    *John 18:15-18, 25b-27*

New Birth Under The Shadow                      27
    *Acts 2:1-15, 32-47*

Boldness And Healing Under The Shadow           43
    *Acts 3:1-10*
    *Acts 4:1-12*

Loyalty Under The Shadow                        61
    *Acts 4:32-37*
    *Acts 5:1-11*

Acceptance Under The Shadow                      75
    *Acts 10:1-23a — Part 1*
    *Acts 10:23b-48 — Part 2*

Praying And Freedom Under The Shadow            97
    *Acts 12:1-5*
    *Acts 12:6-11*
    *Acts 12:12-19*

Postscript                                      109

Epilogue      115
     Simon Peter's Monologue

Bibliography      125

# Foreword

I really don't know whether Simon Peter was a large man from the way my Sunday school teacher always described him to be, or not. But I do know for sure that he cast a very large shadow over the early followers of Jesus and the church regardless of his physical stature.

Forrest Chaffee describes that shadow with solid biblical scholarship, vivid imagery, humor, passion, and delightful narratives saturated with "down home" illustrations from his own childhood, as well as his long experience in parish ministry.

This is a close to the ground, gritty description of one called by Jesus, exposing all his imperfections and strengths. If you rip off his halo given to him by unrealistic romantic pietism you find that marred Peter is us. According to our Bible, he often put his foot in his mouth. He is far from perfect ... but forgiven in huge measure anyway. That makes it such a rich resource for teaching, preaching, and group discussions of all configurations.

As an experienced preacher and professor, I can vision many ways Chaffee's book can be used. I especially think of sermon background material. It might work well to have a brief drama before the sermon portraying the experience you will be talking about. It would also be of use as a Bible study and a discussion group resource. The questions at the end of each chapter are provocative and will ensure lively discussion. I can envision giving the participants a copy and assigning a chapter to be read ahead of time.

In addition to adult forums, someone really in touch with youth culture could also use Chaffee's work for a teenage or young adult Sunday school class discussion helping them to cast the big shadow on their context.

Chaffee appropriately quotes Chrysostom's estimation of Peter, "Peter is the mouthpiece of the disciples, the leader of the apostolic chorus — the pillar of the church, the basis of faith, the foundation of our confession, the worldwide fisherman who brought our race heavenward from the abyss of error." He is right on and thus this work for our edification.

Read on my friend; this is powerful stuff to enlighten and encourage Christians just like you and me. Halfway around the world from where he first cast his shadow and 2,000 years later we, too, can reside in Peter's shadow, whatever his physical size may have been. My Sunday school teacher may have been correct.

> — Jerry L. Schmalenberger
> Retired President, Pacific Lutheran Theological Seminary,
> Berkeley, California

# Prologue

*Guard me as the apple of the eye;*
*hide me in the shadow of your wings....*
— Psalm 17:8

Shadows are an important part of life. Even as a young boy, I was captivated by the shadows around me. My own shadow was an image and shape of myself and early on in life it was amusing to me that my shadow was long in the morning and evening and short at noon. Through the years, when I ran distances in track and cross-country races I would use the sun and my shadow to watch and see if my body was at the right angle and my hands and arms at the right level. Even today, I will use my shadow to check on my golf swing.

As a boy of seven, after the death of my mother from tuberculosis, I went to live with a great-grandmother for a year. Here was a remarkable woman in her eighties who helped support herself by having people stay in her home. In those days, such people were called roomers or boarders. Each had their own room and received both breakfast and supper. One of them was a teacher in the local school system who loved to work with shadows. He showed me how to put my hands into shapes that cast shadows on the wall, everything from butterflies to a mouse, and even the face of an old man.

Close to us lived a neighbor who had a huge backyard with a myriad of flowers and bushes. In the midst of the great garden setting was a sundial. How intrigued I was that you could tell the time of day by the shadow the sun cast because of a metal fixture on a big round stone surface. This surface even had a tilting device that enabled the sundial to show the time for the latitude in which we were living. My teacher friend informed me that this method of telling time was as old as the ancient Greek and Roman civilizations.

9

One grew up in those days singing songs like, "Me And My Shadow" and listening to radio shows that featured frightening stories about a helpful shadow that would cry out in the midst of some evil or danger, "the Shadow knows," and then would laugh boisterously.

Shadows are an important part of our lives today. In the heat of the summer the shadows of shade offer coolness and relief. Our daughter, a psychologist and counselor who works with youth in school systems, says that, in her field, shadows refer to the alter ego of a person, as well as the darker part of ourselves.[1] Even in the sports world, shadows play an important role. Baseball players find it difficult to catch a fly ball in the bright sun and are often equipped with special shaded glasses that they can quickly pull down when the ball is in the air. Batters have a more difficult time hitting when the shadows cover home plate. Even golfers find it harder to putt a ball if shadows cover the hole.[2]

In the Bible, you can find shadows and their symbolism from cover to cover. The heat of the sun was thought to be the work of demonic powers, and shade that offered protection, was the work of a loving and guarding God. In the story of Jonah we read that after preaching to the people of Nineveh he "went out of the city and sat down east of the city, and made a booth for himself there. He sat under it in the shade, waiting to see what would become of the city. The Lord God appointed a bush and made it come up over Jonah, to give shade over his head, to save him from his discomfort, so Jonah was very happy about the bush" (Jonah 4:5-6). When the shade and the bush were taken away, Jonah learned a lesson about God's loving concern for the people of Nineveh. Yes, the Bible speaks of a loving and protecting God and that the shadow of his hand is upon our lives and that we can live under it or run away.

Don Kneeland is the name of an important person in one of the parishes I served as a pastor. Since my mechanical ability was somewhat limited, he was a great asset in my life by often fixing things in our home as well as in the church. He also knew something about interior decorating and was helpful even to the altar guild in the placement of plants. Through it all we became very close friends and had great discussions concerning the faith. How often he would refer to God as the "big hand" in our lives casting a shadow over us of protection and guidance. "Of course," he would say, "you can run away from that shadow."

The Lord our God is pictured as a mighty rock that casts a shadow under which we can be protected and guided. King David speaks of the Lord in a song as one who delivered him from the hand of all his enemies, and from the hand of Saul singing and saying, "The Lord is my rock, my fortress, and my deliverer, my God, my rock, in whom I take refuge" (2 Samuel 22:2-3). It is a common theme in the psalmody and even children today love to sing, "The Lord liveth and blessed be the Rock, and let the God of our salvation be exalted."

God is also pictured as a mighty bird like an eagle telling us that we need to be a people that live under the shadow of his wings. God said to a discouraged Moses, "I bore you on eagles' wings and brought you to myself" (Exodus 19:4). Boaz said to Ruth, "You have found refuge under the wings of God" (Ruth 2:12). The psalmist prays a prayer that should often be breathed from the depth of our being, "Hide me in the shadow of your wings" (Psalm 17:8).

When we were visiting Jerusalem, we walked down the Palm Sunday road that went down through the valley from the Mount of Olives and then up again into the old city. Halfway down there is a chapel, which had been built to mark the place where Jesus wept over the city saying, "Jerusalem, Jerusalem, the city that kills the prophets and stones those who are sent to it! How often have I desired to gather your children together as a hen gathers her brood under her wings, and you were not willing!" (Luke 13:34). This chapel was first built in the twelfth century by the Crusaders, but it quickly fell into ruins after their withdrawal. The present chapel building was built in 1891 and was designed to resemble a tear-shaped shrine. When you enter the chapel you can't help but notice that it is decorated with dark blue colors that produce a somber subdued setting. The altar is framed by a panoramic glass window through which you can see the great city of Jerusalem.[3] We knelt before the altar as a group, praying for Jerusalem and peace and for God's comforting shadow to rest upon our lives.

Often the shadow of God's life-giving power is cast upon us through other people. It can be a loved one or close friend and it can be great people who don't know us but influence us anyway. Even today, if we can get close to a great leader, performer, or athlete we can feel stronger and better. If we can spend even a short time in the shadow of someone great we can be imbued with the power of their life force and personality and in the process become more alive than ever.

Thus, in this book, we want to lift up the life of the disciple Simon Peter. The shadow of this big fisherman is cast upon us through the pages of holy scripture. As we look upon Peter following the days of the resurrection of Jesus as recorded in the book of Acts, we will come under the shadow of his influence and power. Peter who denied Jesus found the great gift of our Lord's forgiveness and acceptance and in the process became a powerful life-giving force in the early church.

This God of ours does not make us come under the shadow of his influence through others. We have the freedom to run away or simply avoid this power. But God is always the mighty hound of heaven[4] bounding, bounding after us, searching for us and longing for us to come under the shadow of his life-giving power.

So we lift up our theme song: More alive under the shadow.

---

1. Carl Jung, *Jung in Christianity* (Princeton: Princeton University Press, 1999). Also found in Eugene Pascal's *Jung To Live By* (New York: Warner Books, Inc., 1992), pp. 136-146.

2. M. Scott Peck, *Golf And The Spirit* (New York: Harmony Books, 1999), pp. 196-197, 247-248.

3. Sami Awwad, *The Holy Land In Colour* (Jerusalem: Palphot Ltd., 1975), p. 32. This book is revised and updated frequently.

4. Imagery from a poem "The Hound of Heaven" by Francis Thompson (1859-1907).

# Forgiveness
# Under The Shadow

*Now Peter was sitting outside in the courtyard. A servant-girl came to him and said, "You also were with Jesus the Galilean." But he denied it before all of them, saying, "I do not know what you are talking about." When he went out to the porch, another servant-girl saw him, and she said to the bystanders, "This man was with Jesus of Nazareth." Again he denied it with an oath, "I do not know the man." After a little while the bystanders came up and said to Peter, "Certainly you are also one of them, for your accent betrays you." Then he began to curse, and he swore an oath, "I do not know the man!" At that moment the cock crowed. Then Peter remembered what Jesus had said: "Before the cock crows, you will deny me three times." And he went out and wept bitterly.* — Matthew 26:69-75

*While Peter was below in the courtyard, one of the servant-girls of the high priest came by. When she saw Peter warming himself, she stared at him and said, "You also were with Jesus, the man from Nazareth." But he denied it, saying, "I do not know or understand what you are talking about." And he went out into the forecourt. Then the cock crowed. And the servant-girl, on seeing him, began again to say to the bystanders, "This man is one of them." But again he denied it. Then after a little while the bystanders again said to Peter, "Certainly you are one of them; for you are a Galilean." But he began to curse, and he swore an oath, "I do not know this man you are talking about." At that moment the cock crowed for the second time. Then Peter remembered that Jesus had said to him, "Before the cock crows twice, you will deny me three times." And he broke down and wept.* — Mark 14:66-72

*Then they seized him and led him away, bringing him into the high priest's house. But Peter was following at a distance. When they had kindled a fire in the middle of the courtyard and sat down together, Peter sat among them. Then a servant-girl, seeing him in the firelight, stared at him and said, "This man also was with him." But he denied it, saying, "Woman, I do not know him." A little later someone else, on seeing him, said, "You also are one of them." But Peter said, "Man, I am not!" Then about an hour later still another kept insisting, "Surely this man also was with him; for he is a Galilean." But Peter said, "Man, I do not know what you are talking about!" At that moment, while he was still speaking, the cock crowed. The Lord turned and looked at Peter. Then Peter remembered the word of the Lord, how he had said to him, "Before the cock crows today, you will deny me three times." And he went out and wept bitterly.*      — Luke 22:54-62


*Simon Peter and another disciple followed Jesus. Since that disciple was known to the high priest, he went with Jesus into the courtyard of the high priest, but Peter was standing outside at the gate. So the other disciple, who was known to the high priest, went out, spoke to the woman who guarded the gate, and brought Peter in. The woman said to Peter, "You are not also one of this man's disciples, are you?" He said, "I am not." Now the slaves and the police had made a charcoal fire because it was cold, and they were standing around it and warming themselves. Peter also was standing with them and warming himself.*

*They asked him, "You are not also one of his disciples, are you?" He denied it and said, "I am not." One of the slaves of the high priest, a relative of the man whose ear Peter had cut off, asked, "Did I not see you in the garden with him?" Again Peter denied it, and at that moment the cock crowed.*
— John 18:15-18, 25b-27

*They shall all know me ... says the Lord; for I will*
*forgive their iniquity, and remember their sin no more.*
— Jeremiah 31:34b


The shadow of a man called Peter stretches out over our lives and shows us how to become more alive with forgiveness.

There are sudden twists and turns in life that cause us to change directions and experience new life. It's an old story that has been making its rounds that tells us about a thief who checked out a certain home for the purpose of robbing it. One night when he knew the owner and family were gone he found an unlocked window. Carefully he opened the window and climbed up over the sill and then let himself down into a room. When his eyes became accustomed to the darkness he found himself staring into the eyes of a Doberman pinscher. The thief froze and waited but nothing happened. Then he was stunned to see a parrot sitting on the head of the dog. He continued to wait but nothing happened. Finally he decided he would go ahead about his business. Taking a cloth sack that had been tucked into his belt he walked into the next room and found some valuable sterling silver that he placed within the sack. The dog followed and the parrot squawked, "You're going to get caught! You're going to get caught!" The thief froze again but nothing happened so he went on through the house finding an expensive vase and some precious jewelry. All the time the dog followed with the parrot squawking in each room, "You're going to get caught!" Finally the thief was so upset at the parrot that he yelled out, "Can't you say anything else you stupid bird?!" Suddenly the parrot squawked, *"Sic-em!"*

What a sudden turn of events must have followed full of crashing and chaos. And our lives can take such sudden turns that it almost takes our breath away. This was true for the apostle Simon Peter whose great shadow stretches across the centuries and rests upon our lives today. Peter became such a dynamic leader and influence on the age in which he lived and, yes, upon our lives today so that to live under his shadow is to become more alive than ever. So let us together take a closer look.

### The Big Fisherman

Simon Peter, known as the big fisherman, was strong and rugged from the pull of the nets and the wind and the waves of the Sea of Galilee. He knew about the fierce storms that would occur suddenly from the swirling winds that would sweep down through the narrow valleys of the rugged hills around the lake. When he was confronted by Jesus and called to be one of his disciples, Simon quickly made the decision to follow and was helped in the process through the encouragement of his brother Andrew. Big, bold, and brash, Peter soon assumed the leadership of the disciples and along with another set of brothers that we know as James and John became a part of an inner circle that was very close to Jesus.

There are three dramatic episodes in the gospels that show this closeness of the inner circle in their relationship to Jesus. One day on the streets of Capernaum, the leader of the local synagogue, a man by the name of Jairus, came running up to Jesus and gasped out the words, "Please come quickly to my home for my daughter is close to death." When Jesus and the crowds approached the home you could hear the shrieking of the mourners announcing the death of the little girl. Jesus then went with only Peter, James, and John along with the weeping parents into the home and came to the little girl and caused her spirit to return so that she lived again!

It was Peter, James, and John who were with Jesus at the time of his transfiguration on the mountainside when the face of Jesus shone as the sun and he was changed into his heavenly glory. Moses and Elijah were seen talking with Jesus and strengthening and encouraging him for his approaching struggles and death in the valley below. In the midst of it all, the voice of God the Father, like thunder itself, was heard proclaiming: "This is my Son, the Beloved; with him I am well pleased; listen to him!" (Matthew 17:5). Peter himself would say later in his ministry, "For we did not follow cleverly devised myths when we made known to you the power and coming of our Lord Jesus Christ, *but we had been eyewitnesses of his majesty*" (2 Peter 1:16 emphasis mine).

Finally it was Peter, James, and John who were with Jesus on the night when he was captured and brought to trial before the Sanhedrin, the governing body of the Jews. After Jesus had spent some time with his disciples in the upper room in Jerusalem and ate with them the Passover meal, they sang a hymn together and then proceeded down into the Kidron Valley and up the slopes of the Mount of Olives to the Garden of Gethsemane. Knowing that death was near, Jesus took Peter, James, and John further with him into the Garden and asked them to watch with him while he wrestled and struggled in prayer. But it was very late and they drifted off to sleep. Three times Jesus came and awakened them and finally he said, "Could you not stay awake with me one hour?" (Matthew 26:40). At that point, the soldiers and priests came and captured Jesus and most of the disciples fled in great fear.

What happens next is difficult to believe and it is an event that has caused some to question the veracity of Peter's faith and to move away from his great shadow. If we look carefully, we discover that this is a universal experience of such truth and power that none of us can ever remain the same.

You will remember that when Jesus and his disciples left the upper room to go to the Garden of Gethsemane, Jesus sighed and said, "You will all become deserters." The answer of Peter is significant and recorded in all the gospels. But since the gospel of Mark is based on the preaching of Peter we hear his answer and the response of Jesus from that record: "Peter said to him, 'Even though all become deserters, I will not.' Jesus said to him, 'Truly, I say to you this day, this very night, before the cock crows twice, you will deny me three times.' But he said vehemently, 'Even though I must die with you, I will not deny you.' And all of them said the same" (Mark 14:29-31). Surely these words and this assurance of Peter to Jesus were not lightly given. Peter spoke them with all of his heart and spirit!

**Broken Promises**

Have you ever made a promise with all your heart and mind and were absolutely convinced that you would never go back on your word? We, too, can make such promises to our children and to those whom we love only to have such promises challenged and overcome by what happens in the sometimes unbelievable twists of life.

17

I certainly discovered the truth of going back on one's word as a young boy. For a time in my life my sister and I were raised by a very strict grandmother. And to this day, I thank God that I was nourished and protected and loved by her after the death of my mom from tuberculosis. We lived in a small town on the rolling prairies of North Dakota in a huge, old home surrounded by a white picket fence with a great grove of cottonwood trees in the back. In the dining room was a large protruding bay window that let in so much light that the room was full of cheerfulness and joy. My sister and I wanted to go outside and play a game that was termed "bat the ball in the air and catch it as soon as you can." There were points that were given on a descending scale depending on whether you caught the ball on the fly, on one bounce, or two. My grandmother made us promise that we would stay away from the house and especially the big bay window. After all, there was an empty lot right across the street where we could play.

When we went outside, other kids were playing in the lot so I said to my sister, "Let's just play here by the house and I'll really be careful and hit away from the house and the bay window." I assured my sister I would watch out for the big bay window, after all, we had made a promise. This worked for a while but suddenly I cut under the ball with the bat and it went behind me — crash! — and smashed right through the bay window. Both of us ran and hid behind an old storage shed. Yes, we had broken our promises and now had to face the music for our actions. To make a long story short, we finally went back into the house with tears running down our cheeks only to discover to our amazement a loving and forgiving grandmother who made us understand what the old saying, "A promise made is a promise kept" really meant. Although broken promises are such a part of our lives, there is a marvelous life-giving force that lifts our spirits and gives us a new start. We call it forgiveness.

We return to the story of the man called Peter who had promised he would not run away but would give up his very life to protect Jesus if he had to. How could this loyal disciple and leader of them all deny ever knowing Jesus? Certainly Peter at times has been maligned and ridiculed as being a weak disciple full of bluster and promises that he could not keep. Yet what happened to Peter could only have happened to someone who possessed tremendous courage. All of the other disciples ran away when Jesus was captured except for Peter and John. They followed him at a distance all the way to the home of the high priest. For them to enter into the courtyard of the high priest's home was like entering into the lion's den. When Peter was confronted by the servant-girl who recognized him as one of the prominent followers of Jesus, you would think that Peter would have fled for his life. Surely there were two emotions in the heart of Peter. On the one hand there was the great fear of danger and death and on the other his all-consuming love for Jesus. Something else gave Peter away when surrounded by the soldiers and servants in the courtyard and that was his accent, for Peter was a Galilean and these people were known for the tough kind of brogue in their speech. It was such an ugly kind of accent that no Galilean was allowed to pronounce the benediction at a worship service in the synagogue![1]

When Peter denied Jesus the third time it was then that he heard the cock crow. William Barclay reminds us that this probably could not have been the sound of a bird. The home of the high priest was in the center of Jerusalem where according to Jewish law no cocks and hens were to be allowed in the city. At 3 a.m., which was the beginning of the fourth watch of the night, there was the changing of the guard at the Fortress of Antonio and everyone was alerted because there would be heard the sound of the trumpet known as the "cock-crow."[2]

We are indebted to the gospel of Luke for adding another aspect to the historical account. At the time of the "cock-crow," a door opened and Jesus was led out by the soldiers and we are told that Jesus turned and looked at Peter. One can imagine Peter speaking of his denial and saying, "In that look there was pain but no indignation. There was disappointment, but there was also forgiveness and love. That look was like a mirror in which I saw myself as I really was — a coward and a traitor. But it was also a window through which I saw the loving heart of this Jesus. Even though I was strong I went out and wept bitterly. Yes, the world knows of my failure and denial, but it also knows of my remorse and repentance."[3] No wonder James Montgomery, the great hymn writer, wrote the words we love to sing:

*In the hour of trial, Jesus, plead for me,*
*Lest by base denial I depart from thee.*
*When thou seest me waver, with a look recall;*
*Nor from fear or favor suffer me to fall.*[4]

Now we raise the question: "How did Peter really know that he was forgiven?" When he went out and wept bitterly he must have been alone. By 3:00 the next afternoon Jesus had been crucified and had died on the cross. And by 6 p.m. on that Friday when the Jewish sabbath began, Jesus had been buried in a cave located in a garden belonging to Joseph of Arimathea. Yes, Jesus was buried and gone. On the Sunday following, there came a knocking on the door and Peter and John were told by the women that the great stone that covered the grave cave of Jesus was rolled away and the body of Jesus was gone. We are told that Peter and John raced for the tomb and John being younger got there first and stood on the outside peering into the tomb. But big and bold Peter brushed by John and entered the tomb. And when their eyes became accustomed to the gloom they saw the grave cloths of Jesus still laying in their folds and the napkin that had been around his head had been taken off, carefully folded, and laid to the side. They saw and wondered if perhaps Jesus was alive! (John 20:1-8).

**Assurance Of Acceptance And Forgiveness**
In this state of wonder, sorrow, and fear, how did Peter come to know that he was forgiven and accepted again? What empowered him to become such a great leader that his shadow rests upon us all? Surely he must have remembered the teachings of Jesus. One day Peter wondered how much he should forgive someone knowing the forgiving nature of Jesus. He knew that the Jewish law stated that one should forgive his brother and neighbor no more than three times. So Peter decided to double the number and add another for good measure. When Peter came to Jesus he asked,

20

"How many times should one forgive another? Is seven times enough?" I'm sure he probably felt pretty smug about saying seven times, and I'm sure he was blown away by the answer of Jesus. "Not seven times, but I tell you, seventy-seven times" (Matthew 18:22). Some translations say, "seventy times seven." In other words, there should be no end to forgiveness.

Once for a children's sermon I asked my daughter to make me some posters so that I could illustrate this message. These were three huge pieces of poster board. One had three colored circle stickers. Another had seven and the third had 490 of them. She must have spent the better part of an afternoon putting them together. You could hardly believe how colorful a poster board with 490 colored circle stickers representing forgiveness looked!

The gospel of John tells us that as time went on after the resurrection the disciples grew more and more restless. Finally some of them decided it was time to go fishing and so they journeyed northward to the Sea of Galilee. How good it was for them to feel the wind and the waves and the pull of the nets. They fished all through the night and caught nothing. In the wee hours of the morning as the mist began to rise along the shore, they saw the figure of a man standing there only about 100 yards away. The man cried out to them, "Have you caught any fish?" When they shouted out that they had caught nothing the man on the shore shouted back, "Let your nets down on the other side of the boat." When they did, the nets enclosed a huge school of fish. It was then that Peter recognized Jesus and leaped into the water and waded ashore.

When all had gathered on the shore, they noticed Jesus had made a breakfast of fish and bread for them. Then when all were standing there in awe Jesus began to ask Peter, "Simon, son of John, do you love me more than these?" In fact, Jesus asked Peter the question three times in a row. Each time Peter said, "Yes, Lord; you know that I love you!" To this answer of Peter Jesus said, "Feed my lambs. Tend my sheep. Feed my sheep." In that moment Peter knew that Jesus was reminding him of his threefold denial, but not only that, Peter just knew that he was forgiven, accepted, and empowered by the forgiveness of our God that cannot be measured and knows no end (John 21:1-18).

21

My friends who read this, I want you to know that to walk in the shadow of Peter is to walk in the shadow of forgiveness and to be more alive than ever. Still, there are times in which it is difficult to receive forgiveness and difficult to forgive someone who has wronged you.

In one of the parishes where I served as a pastor, there were several families who farmed the land and who were strong supporters of the congregation and its mission. Two of these farm families were great friends and always sat together in worship and served in many ways. Their farms were even adjacent to each other. But one day, the two farmers got into a huge dispute over the ownership of some land that was next to both of their farms. This resulted in much ill feeling and there was so much anger between them that they began to give each other the silent treatment. Much to the chagrin of the wives and the children, the two farmers began to avoid each other at all costs. When they came to church they would sit at opposite corners and when it was their turn to usher they made sure they served on different sides. On a communion Sunday, they made sure that they came up to the altar at different tables.

One Sunday when I came to church I caught my breath because I noticed there was a mistake in the scheduling of the ushers. Both of these farmers were to usher on a communion Sunday, which meant that at the time of the distribution both of these farmers would have to walk together down the center aisle, stand there and receive registration cards, and give assistance and directions to the visitors. Needless to say, I was nervous in the worship service and kept praying that the presence of the Spirit would help to keep everything peaceful. When it came time for the communion to be served, both farmers came down the center aisle like stiff soldiers looking only straight ahead with very grim expressions. As the people came forward they would smile and greet these ushers. Some even shook their hands and patted them on the back. All of a sudden, I noticed that one of the farmers whispered to the other and there was a nodding of their heads.

In our communion service when all had received the sacrament, then those who had assisted and served were to kneel at the altar rail and receive the bread and wine. Something incredible happened. The two farmers knelt together and received and when they stood up after the blessing they turned to each other and smiled. Then in front of the entire congregation they hugged each other and there was not a dry eye in the whole group. No doubt about it forgiveness, real forgiveness, flowed between them.

During the years of my ministry, I have been asked three great questions concerning forgiveness over and over again. If we are to walk under the great shadow of God's mercy and forgiveness, we need to wrestle with these questions and have some kind of conviction concerning the truths that are found in their answers.

**1. Doesn't real forgiveness involve forgetting?** If you have been deeply hurt and wronged by another individual it is not possible to forget but it is possible for the hurt to heal over. Trying to pretend that an injury and hurt didn't happen or trying to believe that it doesn't really matter is of course dangerous to our well-being. Repressing a hurtful memory can produce all kinds of problems, even sickness and breakdowns. In the final analysis, I believe that it's not even humanly possible to forget serious injury. "Forgive and forget" is an Old English proverb that dates back to the fourteenth century and it's still not good advice. However, if reconciliation has occurred between two people and it is absolutely genuine over a period of time, the hurting will begin to heal over.

What do the scriptures say to us? For one thing, only God can forgive and forget. How I have loved and committed to memory the words of the psalmist: "The Lord is merciful and gracious, slow to anger and abounding in steadfast love. He does not deal with us according to our sins, nor pay us according to our iniquities. For as the heavens are high above the earth so great is his steadfast love toward those who fear him, as far as the east is from the west, so far he removes our transgressions from us" (Psalm 103:8, 10, 11-12).

**2. Doesn't real forgiveness require the other person who has wronged us to repent?** At this point it is important for us to recognize that it is when we feel deep anger or pain that we begin to live in an emotional climate in which we feel we should withhold forgiveness until the one who has hurt us repents. I agree with

23

those counselors who look at this from another angle. If our forgiveness depends upon another person's repentance then we become a victim again. We are letting the other person control our actions. We hand over considerable power to the one who has hurt us. Maybe it would be helpful if we remember our Lord praying from the cross for his enemies, saying, "Father, forgive them for they know not what they do."

**3. Doesn't real forgiveness come about naturally if we wait long enough?** I don't know if any forgiveness comes about naturally. Forgiveness comes about by an initial decision of really wanting to forgive. It requires a power beyond us, the power of our Lord Jesus Christ, to indwell us to the point that it gives us the ability to *want* to do it. Such forgiveness comes through wanting to begin the process and then it ends up being the work of God's grace in your life and mine.[5]

Yes, the shadow of a man called Peter rests upon our lives, a man who knew something about denial and deep hurts as well as the sorrow of knowing that he had hurt the one he loves the most. Living under his shadow is experiencing the forgiveness and love that flowed from our Lord Jesus to and through Peter and also to and through us today. In this shadow of forgiveness we become more alive than ever.

---

1. William Barclay, *The Gospel of Matthew*, vol. 2 (Philadelphia: Westminster Press, 1957, 1958), p. 382.

2. *Ibid*, pp. 282-283.

3. This is a quote from the monologue on Simon Peter that I have used for over thirty years and is found at the end of this book. Originally it was from a dialogue with Peter circulated among pastors from an unknown source.

4. From the hymn, "In The Hour Of Trial," words by James Montgomery (1771-1854).

5. This thought comes from a sermon on forgiveness by Dan Solomon in Boone, Iowa.

# Reflection And Discussion

## Thought Questions

1. What are the ways in which we as Christians can deny Jesus?

2. Does real forgiveness involve forgetting?

3. Doesn't forgiveness require the other person who has wronged us to repent?

4. Doesn't forgiveness come about naturally if we wait long enough?

## Agree Or Disagree

- The many differences in the accounts of Peter's denial show that the story is false.

- Peter's denial of Jesus shows a real weakness in his character.

- There is a limit to the number of times we should forgive.

- There are some things that are impossible to forgive.

# New Birth
# Under The Shadow

*When the day of Pentecost had come, they were all together in one place. And suddenly from heaven there came a sound like the rush of a violent wind and it filled the entire house where they were sitting. Divided tongues, as of fire, appeared among them, and a tongue rested on each of them. All of them were filled with the Holy Spirit and began to speak in other languages, as the Spirit gave them ability.*

*Now there were devout Jews from every nation under heaven living in Jerusalem. And at this sound the crowd gathered and was bewildered, because each one heard them speaking in the native language of each. Amazed and astonished, they asked, "Are not all these who are speaking Galileans? And how is it that we hear, each of us, in our own native language? Parthians, Medes, Elamites, and residents of Mesopotamia, Judea and Cappadocia, Pontus and Asia, Phrygia and Pamphylia, Egypt and the parts of Libya belonging to Cyrene, and visitors from Rome, both Jews and proselytes, Cretans and Arabs — in our own languages we hear them speaking about God's deeds of power." All were amazed and perplexed, saying to one another, "What does this mean?" But others sneered and said, "They are filled with new wine."*

*But Peter, standing with the eleven, raised his voice and addressed them, "Men of Judea and all who live in Jerusalem, let this be known to you, and listen to what I say. Indeed, these are not drunk, as you suppose, for it is only nine o'clock in the morning."*

*"This Jesus God raised up, and of that all of us are witnesses. Being therefore exalted at the right hand of God, and having received from the Father the promise of the Holy Spirit, he has poured out this that you both*

27

*see and hear. For David did not ascend into the heavens, but he himself says, 'The Lord said to my Lord, "Sit at my right hand, until I make your enemies your footstool." 'Therefore let the entire house of Israel know with certainty that God has made him both Lord and Messiah, this Jesus whom you crucified."*

*Now when they heard this, they were cut to the heart and said to Peter and to the other apostles, "Brothers, what should we do?" Peter said to them, "Repent, and be baptized every one of you in the name of Jesus Christ so that your sins may be forgiven; and you will receive the gift of the Holy Spirit. For the promise is for you, and your children, and for all who are far away, everyone whom the Lord our God calls to him." And he testified with many other arguments and exhorted them, saying, "Save yourselves from this corrupt generation." So those who welcomed his message were baptized, and that day about three thousand persons were added. They devoted themselves to the apostles' teaching and fellowship, to the breaking of bread and the prayers.*

*Awe came upon everyone, because many wonders and signs were being done by the apostles. All who believed were together and had all things in common; they would sell their possessions and goods and distribute the proceeds to all, as any had need. Day by day, as they spent much time together in the temple, they broke bread at home and ate their food with glad and generous hearts, praising God and having the goodwill of all the people. And day by day the Lord added to their number those who were being saved.*

— Acts 2:1-15, 32-47

*You have been born anew, not of perishable*
*but of imperishable seed,*
*through the living and enduring word of God.*
— 1 Peter 1:23

Sometimes we believe that if only we could have enough material possessions and winning scores in life we could become someone really new but our Lord shows us another way and enables us to experience a new birth today.

We remember vividly that Simon Peter, after denying he had ever known Jesus, fled into the darkness and wept bitterly. But when Jesus rose from the dead he sought out Peter. He found him and some of the other disciples on the Sea of Galilee after a night of fishing. At a breakfast of fish and bread that Jesus had prepared, Peter experienced forgiveness and acceptance and a new birth of life. This new birth of life is available to you and to me this and every day. It comes to us from the ever-seeking Jesus under the shadow of Simon Peter stretching through the centuries.

It's an old story but it still relates a message to us today. There was a Sunday school that operated under a particular policy of discipline. If any of the boys and girls became too difficult to handle they were sent to the pastor's office as a last resort. One day, little Johnny became very unruly and uncontrollable and disturbed the whole class so finally he was sent to the pastor's office. The kindly old pastor made Johnny sit down in one of the large chairs and then looked over the lesson materials for the day. Since the lesson told about Jesus ascending into heaven, he asked Johnny, "Where is Jesus?" The little boy was frightened and didn't know what to say. Again the pastor asked, "Where is Jesus? I'm sure you know where he is!"

There was only silence.

Again the pastor asked, "Where is Jesus?"

Suddenly Johnny jumped out of his chair, ran out of the office, down the hallway, out of the building, and all the way home. He ran through the front door and up the stairway and into his room and slammed the door. The mother was startled and after waiting and listening she ran up the stairs and opened the door. There was Johnny sitting on the edge of his bed.

"Johnny," she said, "Why did you come home from Sunday school? What happened?"

"Mom," Johnny replied, "we're in deep trouble. That church has lost Jesus and they think we know where he is!"

29

We do know where Jesus is today. Certainly, he is in heaven but he is also with each of us through the power of the Spirit. After Jesus rose from the dead and just before his ascension into heaven, he met with his disciples on the Mount of Olives and told them, "You will receive power when the Holy Spirit has come upon you; and you will be my witnesses in Jerusalem, in all Judea and Samaria, and to the ends of the earth" (Acts 1:8). At that point, we read that Jesus was "lifted up, and a cloud took him out of their sight." Once again, the disciples felt very much alone and so they walked down the Mount of Olives, through the narrow Kidron Valley, and then up into the city of Jerusalem. They found some of the other followers and they met together in the home of the upper room.

**The Waiting And Watching Fellowship**
We are told there were 120 of these followers (Acts 1:15). This included the disciples, without Judas Iscariot, and the women who went to the empty tomb on resurrection morning. Luke tells us they were "Mary Magdalene, Joanna, and Mary, the mother of James, and the other women who were with them" (Luke 24:10). Also in that group there must have been Mary, the mother of Jesus, along with Jesus' brothers and sisters. I also would like to believe that Nicodemus who came to the cross with 100 pounds of myrrh and aloe to anoint the body of Jesus was there, as well as Joseph of Arimathea. There were also Joseph called Barsabbas, also known as Justus, and a man called Matthias (Acts 1:23).

Is it not possible that Bartimaeus, the blind man on the Jericho road, who called out to Jesus and received his sight was there? Certainly, the gospel of Mark remembers his very name and states that he followed Jesus all the way to Jerusalem and the cross (Mark 10:46-52). Yes, it is easy to surmise that Lazarus, who was raised by Jesus from the dead, was with the group in the upper room. After all, he and his sisters, Mary and Martha, were the closest of friends with Jesus. And when Lazarus was raised from the dead he became like a celebrity in the Jerusalem area and caused many to believe in Jesus (John 12:9-11).

What a great mixture of followers! We know that they prayed and worshiped together, conducted some important business, and watched and waited. There must have been many questions to be considered and feelings to work through. I agree with Lloyd Ogilvie who writes:

> *Had the disciples ever worked through their real feelings about a person like Mary Magdalene? With Jesus' absence, they were confronted by the fact that their relationship always had been cushioned with His gracious acceptance. Did they feel as He did? And what about the Pharisee, Nicodemus? Was he really one of them? He was a member of the Sanhedrin and yet had not been able to stop the excruciating thing the Jewish leaders had done to the Lord. The Pharisee had shown his loyalty by asking for the body of Jesus and assisted in His burial. But could he be trusted? And what about rich Joseph of Arimathea? He provided the tomb in the garden outside the city wall. But with all that Jesus had said about the rich and the responsibility for the poor, was his presence a genuine concern? If he had provided the tomb, probably as a secret admirer and follower of the Lord, was he really to be accepted among the inner band of loyal followers?*[1]

In the midst of all their questions and emotions, I have to believe that their common grief and fear brought them together and enabled them to pray together. Prayer is a powerful resource in our meetings together and certainly can bring about unity. Often have I seen it in a contentious gathering of people meeting together — when they were able to pray together there was a power that cleared the air, sharpened the mind, and softened the heart so that something was accomplished.

During the time that 120 followers were together, the shadow of Peter's leadership spread over the group. There was a need to choose another disciple to take the place of Judas and it was Peter who kept the group together and initiated the process of selection.

**The Day Of Pentecost**

Ten days went by! Then came the day of Pentecost, one of the three great festivals along with Passover and the Feast of Tabernacles, in which every male Jew within twenty miles of Jerusalem was legally bound to attend. The word "Pentecost" means "fiftieth" and occurred fifty days after the Passover in the month of June. It celebrated the early harvest of grain and the giving of the law to Moses on Mount Sinai. Since the weather would have been warm and beautiful and conducive to travel, the Jews from all around the Mediterranean world would have made the journey to the holy city of Jerusalem. Something incredible happened that caused a great crowd of people to gather around the home in which were the disciples of Jesus and their friends and supporters. The elements that went into this special coming of the power of the Holy Spirit consisted of wind, fire, and other tongues, so let's take a closer look.

**Wind** — On the day of Pentecost there was heard the sound of a violent wind, only the wind was not felt. As a boy growing up on the prairies of North Dakota, the wind was always blowing. Sometimes the wind was just a gentle breeze that cooled the home on a hot summer day. The wind enabled one to fly a kite and to listen to those tinkling chimes that hung in the porch that would lull one to sleep. The wind could be a great friend.

Every summer I would spend some time on a farm owned by the Matthew family who had a son my age. What great fun we had playing in the huge grove of trees on the north side of the farmstead that served as a windbreak for the winter storms. It was a hot, sultry evening and I was seated on the back step, hoping for a cooling breeze. Two miles to the south was a neighboring farmstead that had a great grove of lilacs on one side that were in full bloom. Though it didn't seem like the breeze was stirring, suddenly there came to my senses the distinct perfumed sweet smell of the lilacs, yes, from two miles away. I realized that the air was moving and stirring and so it is with the power of the Spirit.

The wind can also be a mighty force. Hurricanes roar inland and destroy homes and communities. Almost without warning, thunderstorms roll into town or across a lake and catch one by surprise and do much damage. Those who live by an ocean know that the surf can be up and the waves pound wickedly, sending the sailboat toward the rocks. The wind can be a fierce and mighty power and so it is with the power of the Spirit.

On the day of Pentecost, there came from the heavens the sound and roaring of the wind that was heard within the home where the 120 were gathered, as well as in the streets of Jerusalem, but the wind was not felt. This coming of the wind was the coming of the power of the Spirit. In the Greek language of the Bible the word for the Spirit is *ruach*. When you pronounce this word properly you utter a guttural sound with breath in each syllable — "REW! ACK!" Jesus knew all about the wind of the Spirit and how to pronounce this word. In his conversation with Nicodemus, the Pharisee, in the darkness of the night, Jesus said to him, "The wind blows where it chooses, and you hear the sound of it, but you do not know where it comes from or where it goes. So it is with everyone who is born of the Spirit" (John 3:8).

**Fire** — A second element that shows the coming of the power of the Spirit on those first followers of Jesus on the day of Pentecost was fire. We are told that "divided tongues, as of fire, appeared among them, and a tongue rested on each of them" (Acts 2:3). Often in the historical record of the scriptures, thunder, lightning, and fire are associated with the presence of the Lord our God. When God wanted to call Moses to lead the people out of the slavery of Egypt he spoke to him out of a burning bush, only the bush was never consumed. When the people of Israel left the slavery of Egypt there went before them a cloud by day and a pillar of fire by night for God was with them. When God came to Moses on Mount Sinai to give him the Ten Commandments we read, "Now Mount Sinai was wrapped in smoke, because the Lord had descended upon it in fire; the smoke went up like the smoke of a kiln, while the whole mountain shook violently" (Exodus 19:18).

Fiery lightning and storms were a great part of my life as a child. In fact, there are thunderstorms full of lightning that are always found all over the earth. Scientists tell us that there are an estimated 2,000 thunderstorms going on in the world at any one time! Often in the evenings, the heat lightning would seemingly move along the ground by the great fields of wheat. Late in the

33

afternoons, huge cumulonimbus clouds called thunderheads would form and billow up into the sky some 50,000 feet. They would flash with lightning and you could hear the roll of thunder. Many of you have done the same thing as I have done through the years when there is an approaching thunderstorm. When I would see the lightning I would begin to count, "one thousand one, one thousand two," until there was heard the thunder because each second of time that one would count off between seeing the lightning and hearing its thunder would equal approximately one mile of distance. I would do this even when playing golf so I would know when to get off the course!

The story is told of a farm family in the midst of a thunderstorm. It was dark and it was time for their little boy to go to bed. The lightning was flashing and the thunder was crashing and the boy was very frightened. The parents decided that he could stay for a while and they let him sit between them as they read to him has favorite storybook. Finally, even though the thunderstorm continued, the mom picked him up and carried him up the stairs to his bedroom. The mom tucked him in and told him not to be afraid because God was with him. Back downstairs, the mom was sitting with her husband when suddenly there was a horrific crash of thunder that shook the whole house. Then they heard their son jumping out of bed and coming down the hallway to the head of the stairs.

"Go back to bed, God is with you," said the dad.

The little boy quickly replied, "No, I am coming down to be with mom. Dad, you come up here and be with God!"

On the day of Pentecost in the city of Jerusalem there was the roaring sound of the wind and the disciples and their friends and followers, all 120 of them, came out into the street with single tongues of fire upon their heads. Someone has written that if the resurrection of Jesus was like lightning, then the day of Pentecost was the thunder that followed.

Now the fire and the mighty roaring in the sky caused a great crowd of people to gather together in the street by the home of the upper room. What happened next is a further demonstration of the power of the Spirit.

**Other Tongues** — Since it was the great festival of Pentecost, there were people gathered from all around the Mediterranean Sea and we read that the disciples and their followers spoke to them "in the native language of each" (Acts 2:6). No matter what country and area they were from, they could understand the message that was given. What happened here was not the phenomenon of "speaking in tongues," which occurred later in the church and was like a babbling of one's mouth involuntarily because of incredible ecstatic emotions from the indwelling of the Spirit and required special interpreters. Certainly, we will deal with this later on in this book as we continue to follow the shadow of Simon Peter. What we have here is simply a speaking in "other tongues." All of the Jews around the Mediterranean Sea could speak a language called Aramaic. This was the spoken language and many of the Jews also knew the Greek language that was the written language in the business world. The people that were speaking in "other tongues" were Galileans who had a very special dialect and brogue that made it difficult for them to be understood. We have already seen how Simon Peter was recognized in the courtyard of the high priest because of his Galilean brogue. The Jews gathered in the streets of the city were from all kinds of countries and areas that had their own kind of dialect yet they could all understand the message that was being given by the disciples and their followers. What a miracle![2]

My grandmother, who raised me after the death of my mom, had come to this country from the northern part of Norway. She could speak Norwegian fluently as well as English and she made no attempt to teach us Norwegian because she wanted us to speak the language of her adopted country. Yet, we would often ask her to speak in Norwegian and tried to learn some things on our own. Her English, though fluent, still contained a distinct accent and brogue that made it difficult at times for us to understand. This memory helps me to understand better the great miracle of "other tongues" that occurred on that day of Pentecost. In some of that crowd were those who had difficulty understanding the miracle of "other tongues" that was going on around them. They sneered and yelled out that the disciples were drunk with new wine!

All eyes were upon Simon Peter who stood before them and began to preach. His shadow is upon our lives as he delivered the first recorded and documented Christian sermon in history. It began with an answer to those who thought he and others were drunk. Peter told the crowd this couldn't possibly be true since it was only 9 a.m. in the morning. The Jewish people would normally have their breakfast at 10 a.m., so it was like Peter was saying, "We haven't even had breakfast yet so we haven't done any drinking!" This sermon was probably only a summary of what was said but we still have here the meat of the message given in less than 600 words. How well I remember when I began my ministry that an old experienced preacher friend said to me, "Remember a real good sermon has an excellent introduction and a great conclusion and the two are close together."

As Peter continues with his message we find here all of the elements that need to be in great preaching today:

1.  First of all, it is **Christ centered**, that is to say, it speaks of the life, death, and resurrection of Jesus as well as his immanent presence among us through the power of the Spirit.
2.  Then the sermon is full of **God's plan** for you and me. Our new birth of life is always available and renewable each day. It comes to us through the death and resurrection of this Jesus and nothing could have been done to stop or alter this carrying out of God's will. It was God's plan and he did it!
3.  Peter's sermon is full of **God's grace** emphasizing that this plan from the beginning was to bring us under the influence of God's love and forgiveness available to us as a wondrous gift.
4.  Finally this sermon contains **an invitation** to the congregation of people gathered. Certainly, this is true of every great sermon throughout all of history. It is an invitation to renew one's relationship to Jesus or to begin a relationship to Jesus requiring a complete turning around of life by the power of the Spirit. This is indeed a new birth under the shadow of Simon Peter.

This sermon of Peter, quoted from the Jewish scriptures, is our Old Testament today. Peter, by quoting from the psalmody as well as the prophet Joel, showed the great crowd and us who listen today that this Jesus is indeed the promised Messiah. Peter concludes, "Therefore let the entire house of Israel know with certainty that God has made him both Lord and Messiah, this Jesus whom you crucified" (Acts 2:36). Obviously, Peter, now assured of his own forgiveness and filled with the gift of courage, reached the hearts of his listeners.

During my undergraduate days at Gustavus Adolphus College in Minnesota, I became a part of one of several teams of students who went out to congregations to lead worship when the pastor for some reason couldn't be in the congregation. Each team had four students: one to make announcements and lead the worship, one to read the liturgy and two of the lessons, one to bring special music, and one to read the gospel and preach. The first assignment that was offered our team was to go to a congregation in the city of Brainerd located in northern Minnesota. This was in the month of January so the weather that weekend was snowy, icy, and bitterly cold. My task was to lead the liturgy and read two lessons of scripture. As we drove along, I could feel myself becoming more and more nervous and uneasy. What on earth had possessed me to take on such an assignment?

When we arrived, we were quite amazed that the church was full of people in spite of the bitter cold. During the worship, I was so nervous that I had great difficulty pronouncing any words beginning with "B" or "P" because of my trembling lips, but somehow I stuttered my way through. Afterward, I was really down on myself and was absolutely certain that I was not meant to be a pastor. As we were greeting the people, a distinguished old man with a great shock of white hair came up to me. He put his arm around my shoulders and said, "Son, you did a great job today in spite of your nervousness. It took great courage for you to help lead a worship service and I guarantee you that you will do better. In fact, you have a very special spirit and I just know that you are destined to be a great pastor! Always be strong and of good courage!" Then to top it off, he gave me a great hug and walked away.

Something happened in that moment that was to follow me all the days of my life. There was received into the heart of my being the gift of courage and inspiration that came through the encouragement of that old man. Wow! I left the church walking on air! My friends who read this, close to you today there is someone who needs a word of encouragement from you. Always remember that encouragement puts courage into the heart of the one who receives it.

No question about it, Simon Peter was full of the Spirit and full of courage and he was able to preach such a sermon that we are told that it "cut to the heart" many of those who heard it to the point that they cried out to Peter and the apostles, "Brothers, what should we do?" (Acts 2:37). At this moment, Peter first of all told them that they needed to repent.

Here is a marvelous word from the Greek word *metanoeo*. In this little word are two words that show us the meaning. The word *meta*, which means "after," and the word *neo* from the word *nous*, which means "the mind." A good definition for repentance is "to change one's mind" and to change one's mind results in a change of direction for our lives. Peter went on to say that not only did the people need to repent, they also needed to be baptized in the name of Jesus Christ. The call to be baptized must have been shocking to them because baptism had been used for those who wanted to become a part of the Jewish faith. It was an initiation into Judaism. John the Baptist had used baptism in the River Jordan for people who wanted to renew their lives and in a sense to be born again to a whole new kind of life. It symbolized a new relationship to the Lord our God. Under the shadow of Peter and the power of the Spirit, 3,000 people were baptized and the early Christian church began. And what a church it was! The qualities of this church are clearly given to us in the historical record and to me describe what any dynamic church is today. So we can say that the church is:

- a people who have a sure knowledge of salvation through Christ's death and resurrection and who have received the living presence of thc Spirit;

- a people who are willing to meet together to study and hear the preaching of the word;
- a people who genuinely care for one another and share much with those in need;
- a people who share together common meals and prayers; and
- a people who are full of praise and joy.

To be honest, I have never seen a great congregation or Christian that wasn't full of praise and the wondrous gift of joy. One of my favorite authors, Robert Louis Stevenson, who wrote such masterpieces as *Kidnapped* and *Treasure Island*, said: "Show me your praises and I will think more of your prayers."[3]

One of the heroes in my life is a basketball coach by the name of John Wooden, who is now in his nineties. He is well aware of the new birth and new life that comes to us through Jesus Christ our Lord. This story comes from an unknown sportswriter.

First of all, his life is marked by faithfulness to his wife, Nellie, who has gone to be with our Lord. When someone talks to him he is quick to say how much he misses her and loves her and can't wait to see her again. On day 21 of every month he will sit down and pen a love letter to what he calls his "best girl, Nellie." Then he will fold it once, slide it in a little envelope, and walk into his bedroom. He then goes to the stack of love letters sitting there on the pillow, unties the yellow ribbon, places the new one on top, and ties the ribbon again. It has been over fifteen years since Nellie died, after a marriage of 53 years. Wow! That means over 180 love letters have been written. In her memory, he sleeps only on his half of the bed, only on his pillow, only on top of the sheets, never between; with just the old bedspread they shared to keep him warm.

John Wooden's life is also marked by his faithfulness to coaching and to those whom he coached. Many of you will remember the years he coached basketball at UCLA, where he had ten NCAA basketball championships, the last in 1975. Nobody has even come within six of them. During his coaching career, he won 88 straight games between January 30, 1971, and January 17, 1974, and nobody has come within 42 games of that record since.

His life is marked by faithfulness to teaching young men to become something great with their whole lives. If you would visit him in his little condo in Encino, twenty minutes northwest of Los Angeles, you would see the report cards of his great-grandchildren and dozens of pictures of his beloved Nellie. And you would hear him say things like "Gracious sakes alive!" and tell stories about teaching "Lewis" the hook shot; Lewis Alcindor, that is, the one who became Kareem Abdul-Jabbar. He is remembered for spending a half hour the first day of practice teaching his men how to put on a sock. "Wrinkles can lead to blisters," he'd warn. Those huge players would sneak looks at one another and roll their eyes. Eventually, they'd do it right. "Good," he'd say, "and now the other foot!"

Of the 180 players who played for him, Wooden knows the whereabouts of 172. Of course, it's not hard when most of them call, checking on his health, secretly hoping to hear some of his simple life lessons so that they can write them on the lunch bags of their children, who will roll *their* eyes.

Though John Wooden is older and his steps are smaller and his back more hunched, he radiates the faith that is still born anew in his heart each day. With that great smile of his he says, "I'm not afraid to die. Death is my only chance to be with Nellie again."

As you and I seek to be born anew each day under the great shadow of Simon Peter, we can nod in agreement with John Wooden as he says, "There is only one kind of life that truly wins, and that's the one that places faith in the hands of the Savior. Until that is done, we are on an aimless course that runs in circles nowhere. Material possessions, winning scores, are meaningless in the eyes of the Lord, because he knows who and what we really are and that is all that matters." Furthermore, he knows what we can become under the shadow of Peter!

Read on to see the great healing power of Jesus coming through Peter and John and their great courage and boldness in the face of a growing opposition.

1. Lloyd J. Ogilvie, *The Communicator's Commentary — Acts* (Waco: Word Books, 1983), p. 47.

2. William Barclay, *The Acts of the Apostles* (Philadelphia: The Westminster Press, 1955), pp. 14-27.

3. Robert Louis Stevenson, *A Child's Garden of Verses* (Edinburgh: Main Stream Publishing Company, 2001), p. 32.

# Reflection And Discussion

**Thought Questions**

1. How does one become a member of the church today?

2. In what ways does new birth involve **wind, fire,** and **other tongues** for our lives?

3. What were the miracles that occurred on the day of Pentecost?

4. What are the characteristics of a dynamic church today?


**Agree Or Disagree**

- Repentance is an act always accompanied by sorrow.

- Baptism should be by immersion.

- Once baptized, always baptized.

- Once baptized, always saved.

# Boldness And Healing Under The Shadow

*One day Peter and John were going up to the temple at the hour of prayer, at three o'clock in the afternoon. And a man lame from birth was being carried in. People would lay him daily at the gate of the temple called the Beautiful Gate so that he could ask for alms from those entering the temple. When he saw Peter and John about to go into the temple, he asked them for alms. Peter looked intently at him, as did John, and said "Look at us." And he fixed his attention on them, expecting to receive something from them. But Peter said, "I have no silver or gold, but what I have I give you; in the name of Jesus Christ of Nazareth, stand up and walk." And he took him by the right hand and raised him up; and immediately his feet and ankles were made strong. Jumping up, he stood and began to walk, and he entered the temple with them, walking and leaping and praising God. All the people saw him walking and praising God, and they recognized him as the one who used to sit and ask for alms at the Beautiful Gate of the temple; and they were filled with wonder and amazement at what had happened to him.* — Acts 3:1-10

*While Peter and John were speaking to the people, the priests, the captain of the temple, and the Sadducees came to them, much annoyed because they were teaching the people and proclaiming that in Jesus there is the resurrection of the dead. So they arrested them and put them in custody until the next day, for it was already evening. But many of those who heard the word believed; and they numbered about five thousand.*

*The next day their rulers, elders, and scribes assembled in Jerusalem, with Annas the high priest, Caiaphas, John, and Alexander, and all who were of*

*the high-priestly family. When they had made the pris-*
*oners stand in their midst, they inquired, "By what*
*power or by what name did you do this?" Then Peter,*
*filled with the Holy Spirit, said to them, "Rulers of the*
*people and elders, if we are questioned today because*
*of a good deed done to someone who was sick and are*
*asked how this man has been healed, let it be known to*
*all of you, and to all the people of Israel, that this man*
*is standing before you in good health by the name of*
*Jesus Christ of Nazareth, whom you crucified, whom*
*God raised from the dead. This Jesus is 'the stone that*
*was rejected by you, the builders; it has become the*
*cornerstone.' There is salvation in no one else, for there*
*is no other name under heaven given among mortals*
*by which we must be saved."*          — Acts 4:1-12

*And this is the boldness we have in him, that if we*
*ask anything according to his will, he hears us.*
          — 1 John 5:14

We know that a shadow is a region of darkness where light is blocked. When the light of the sun is behind us our bodies cast a shadow and the lower the sun is in the sky the longer the shadow. Our shadows are the smallest during the year on the first day of summer around June 21 when the day is the longest and the sun is the highest in the sky. Simon Peter's leadership in the church symbolically casts a shadow down to us today and behind that shadow is the light and power of the living Jesus, our Lord.

From the time that I was a young boy, I have been fascinated with shadows, even my own. One of my favorite authors is Robert Louis Stevenson (1850-1894) who was a Scottish author more than 100 years ago. Early in life, I eagerly read and was royally entertained by his books, such as *Treasure Island*, *Kidnapped*, and *The Strange Case of Dr. Jekyll and Mr. Hyde*. I also enjoyed his poems in *A Child's Garden of Verses* that were different from most poems of his day. Stevenson used simple words and wrote about everyday

44

happenings in a child's life. Before that, children's poems taught lessons in a serious way. Of course I enjoyed his poem titled "My Shadow."

*I have a little shadow that goes in and out with me,*
*And what can be the use of him is more than I can see.*
*He is very, very like me from the heels up to the head;*
*And I see him jump before me, when I jump into my*
*bed.*

*The funniest thing about him is the way he likes to*
*grow —*
*Not at all like proper children, which is always very*
*slow;*
*For he sometimes shoots up taller like an India-rubber*
*ball,*
*And he sometimes goes so little that there's none of him*
*at all.*

*He hasn't got a notion of how children ought to play,*
*And can only make a fool of me in every sort of way.*
*He stays so close behind me, he's a coward you can*
*see;*
*I'd think shame to stick to nursie as that shadow sticks*
*to me!*

*One morning, very early, before the sun was up,*
*I rose and found the shining dew on every buttercup;*
*But my lazy little shadow, like an arrant sleepy-head,*
*Had stayed at home behind me and was fast asleep in*
*bed.*[1]

## The Beggar, Lame From Birth

Under the shadow of Simon Peter's influence and words, we can experience great healing power in our lives even today, so we take a closer look at a miracle of healing that occurred under the shadow of Peter and John. Such a healing stirred up the whole city of Jerusalem and greatly disturbed the religious authorities.

For the devout Jew in those days, there were three special times of prayer occurring in the temple at 9:00 in the morning, noon, and at 3:00 in the afternoon. To their way of thinking, prayer was always beneficial and especially precious and powerful if offered in the temple courts. Since the apostles kept up the customs and the habits in which they were trained, we find Peter and John coming to the temple courts at 3:00 in the afternoon.

Every day there was a beggar, lame from birth, who was carried into the courts of the temple so he could be placed by a gate of the temple called the Beautiful Gate. Most biblical authorities associate this gate with the Nicanor Gate sometimes referred to as the Corinthian Gate because it was made with Corinthian bronze. This magnificent Beautiful Gate served as an entrance between the Court of the Gentiles and the Court of the Women. The doors alone of the gate were forty cubits high and the gate itself fifty cubits. In those days, a cubit was the distance from your elbow to the tip of your middle finger, which in most adults is approximately eighteen inches. I took a yardstick and my cubit was eighteen inches and that of my wife was seventeen-and-a-half inches. So when I calculated the cubits into feet I was rather startled because according to the number of cubits the doors of this gate would have been sixty feet high and the gate itself would have been 75 feet high! Why, that's the height of a seven-story building today.[2] This magnificent gate made of bronze was covered with gold leaf, and how it must have sparkled in the sun!

There was a reason of course why the lame man was carried to this gate of the temple every day. The traffic of people coming and going to the temple would have been numerous and they would because of their time of prayer be more sensitive to the cries of the lame beggar. I have discovered that people in worship today can become quite generous when asked for special offerings for special needs.

Beggars are alive in this day and age, especially in the heart of our cities. In the crosswalks of downtown Minneapolis, there are still beggars who are desperate for help even if it is just money for their next bottle of cheap wine. In fact, if for some reason I am not carrying any cash and I spot a beggar I will not look at them because if they catch your eye they will be most certain to come up to you for help. How well I remember serving a parish located in the inner city of Minneapolis around which were some crumbling neighborhoods that could easily be termed the "slums" where many poor and desperate people lived. They came to our churches so often begging for funds for food that as pastors we decided together to set up a "food pantry" with special days and hours to help the people. How generous the people of the congregations were in donating food as well as clothing. Jesus was right on when he said, "You always have the poor with you, and you can show kindness to them whenever you wish" (Mark 14:7).

Now the lame man would have been well known throughout Jerusalem. According to the historical account, he was over forty years of age and had to be carried to the temple area daily (Acts 3:2; 4:22). The author of this account is the physician, Luke, and in the original Greek you discover that as he describes the physical condition of the lame beggar he uses medical terms. W. K. Hobart writes, "The words used to describe the seat of the lameness tend to show that the writer was acquainted with medical phraseology and had investigated the nature of the disease under which the man suffered."[3] The anklebones of this man from the time that he was born were out of place and he was unable to walk all the years of his life resulting in a paralysis in the heels of his feet and in the sockets of the ankles. This lame man cried out for alms and the Greek text indicates that he called out in a repeated appeal, which he had shouted out for years like some kind of chant. When the beggar saw the approach of Peter and John he heightened his chant.

What happened next is an amazing transformation. We are told Peter and John looked intently at the beggar and Peter said, "Look at us." Obviously they wanted the full attention of the lame man who was calling out to the others passing by. Then Peter said, "I have no silver or gold, but what I have I give you; in the name of Jesus Christ of Nazareth, stand up and walk." They had no alms to give but they had something else that was greater than silver or gold and something more beautiful than the magnificent gate nearby. One cannot help but notice the attention given here to every detail as we are told that Peter used his "right hand" to lift up the lame man. Immediately, his feet and ankles became strong and pliable. What a sight! Suddenly, the man is leaping and walking and walking and leaping and praising God. The crowds of people were full of wonder and amazement. Yes, the commotion and the shouting attracted a larger and larger crowd, and Peter used the opportunity to bear witness to the power of Jesus who had risen from the dead and healing had occurred through the power of the Spirit and in the name of Jesus. So Peter declared that faith in the presence of Jesus and in his name has "made this man strong, whom you see and know; and the faith that is through Jesus has given him this perfect health in the presence of all of you" (Acts 3:16).

We read further that this miracle of healing excited the whole city and upset the leaders. Since the lame man was so well known, no one, not even the Jewish leaders, could deny that a miracle of healing had occurred. At this moment, as Peter was speaking, the captain of the temple and the Sadducees arrived. They were much annoyed, to say the least, because Peter and John were proclaiming with great boldness that in Jesus there was the resurrection of the dead; so they arrested Peter and John and placed them in custody until the next day, since it was now evening.

Early the next day the rulers, elders, and scribes assembled in Jerusalem along with all the high priests and together they asked the prisoners Peter and John to be silent about this Jesus. These leaders could not deny that a miracle of healing occurred because they all could see that a lame and paralyzed man who had lived among them for over forty years was now healthy and walking and leaping and running among them. Peter and John said to the leaders when they were told to be silent about Jesus, "We cannot keep from speaking about what we have seen and heard." At this point nothing could be done to punish Peter and John "because of the people, for all of them praised God for what had happened" (Acts 4:19-21).

## Courage In The Face Of Danger

One is impressed with the courage and boldness of Peter and John because these leaders before whom they had appeared had the power to imprison them and punish them severely. It wouldn't be long before they would have Stephen, one of the first deacons in the early church, stoned publicly for his witness and testimony to Jesus as the promised one of the ages (Acts 7). Courage and boldness are among the gifts of the Spirit in our lives and such gifts enable us to be more alive than ever. The opportunity to show courage can come upon us in a sudden moment of danger.

Wesley Autrey is the name of a fifty-year-old construction worker and the father of three who lived in the city of New York. He was waiting for a downtown subway train when he saw Cameron Hollopeter, a nineteen-year-old student suffering from some kind of medical problem. After stumbling down the platform, Hollopeter, of Littleton, Massachusetts, fell into the tracks with a subway train on its way into the station bearing down on him. Without hesitation, and with a burst of courage, Autrey jumped down to the tracks and rolled with the young man into the trough between the tracks and laid on top of him pressing him down and protecting him as the train rolled over them.

Metropolitan Transportation Authority Executive Director Elliot Sander called Autrey's action "a death-defying act of bravery. We truly have not seen anything like this ... He was at the right place at the right time and did the right thing."

At a city hall news conference, Mayor Michael Bloomberg called Wesley "the hero of Harlem" and presented him with a bronze medallion, the city's highest award for civic achievement. Autrey became an instant celebrity and was given a trip to Disney World and $10,000 from Donald Trump. He received national attention through the news media and was called a representation and symbol of the courage of New Yorkers. When asked about his new celebrity status Autrey replied, "Good things happen when you do good."[4]

We return to our story and affirm again that the shadow of those first apostles and Simon Peter and their boldness and courage rests upon us today. Miracles of healing did happen and not even the Sanhedrin, the governing body of the Jewish could deny it.

Yet, what do we feel about miracles of healing today? Surely, one of the great debilitating delusions among us today is that the great healing and working of miracles ended when the Apostolic Age came to an end. But Jesus our Lord is the same and the needs of the people today are not much different from the first century. I agree with Lloyd Ogilvie, the chaplain of the United States Senate, when he wrote, "The early church discovered through experience that the Lord had called them to preach, teach, and heal in His name. When the Spirit of the Lord is given full reign in a congregation, there will be healings of people's spiritual, psychological, and physical needs. When we preach and teach Christ and pray for people's needs, miracles do happen. And the greatest miracle is the transformation of a person from self-centeredness to Christ-centeredness."[5]

As I write this, there is a silly story making its rounds again that I have loved to tell in the past (and still do!) to make a particular point. Two hikers were walking through the woods to find a place to camp out for the night when they came into a clearing with a huge hole in the ground surrounded by a small brick wall. They came to the edge and noticed that the hole was very dark and they couldn't see the bottom. Curious, they picked up some pebbles on the ground and threw them into the hole and listened for them to hit the bottom. Hearing nothing, they began to believe that the hole was deeper than they thought, so they found a good-sized boulder and dragged it, lifted it up over the wall, and dropped it into the hole. Once again, they listened intently and heard nothing. "Wow," they said, "this hole must be very, very deep." Looking around the clearing they found a railroad tie, so they dragged it over to the hole, lifted it up, and dropped it into the hole. They listened and listened and heard nothing. Suddenly, there came running out of the nearby woods a goat that leaped way up in the air and flew down into the hole. As they were standing there absolutely stunned, a farmer came running out of the woods and called out to the hikers, "Have you seen my goat? I've lost my goat!"

The hikers explained that they had seen a goat running out of the woods and then leaping high into the air and then down into the hole. "Wow," they said, "we have never seen such a sight!"

The farmer quickly replied, "Well, that couldn't have been my goat. You see, my goat was tied to a railroad tie!"

Such a silly, old story highlights the importance of being connected in this life. Certainly we need to be connected to the Lord our God and to each other. Jesus himself, in a discourse to his disciples in that upper room in Jerusalem on the night before he died, said: "Abide in me as I abide in you. Just as the branch cannot bear fruit by itself unless it abides in the vine, neither can you unless you abide in me. I am the vine, you are the branches. Those who abide in me and I in them bear much fruit, because apart from me you can do nothing" (John 15:4-5).

We affirm here that great are the healing miracles of the Lord our God under the shadow of the first apostles and under the shadow of the leadership of Simon Peter. The age of miracles has not come to an end but remains among us today. Surely the Lord our God has chosen many channels through which to bring us miracles of healing today.

**Some Channels Of Healing Today**

A recent newspaper article indicated a "thumbs down" on America for losing to England when it comes to health and that we should be ashamed to think that a country like England whose people are stereotypically thought of as pasty-skinned and inclined to eat fish and chips every day could beat out the supposedly robust Americans. In the study, no one was sure why the English are healthier, but experts in the areas of nutrition and exercise state that Americans exercise too little, have too much stress, and too little money for health care. Of course, it should also be noted that England has a nationalized health care system.

What stunned me was the fact that not only is England ahead of us, but the World Health Organization reports that the United States ranks behind two dozen other countries (including Canada) when it comes to health. Our health care crisis is no secret. One of the writers of the study stated that "not only is the problem growing bigger, now it's bloody embarrassing."[6]

Jesus our Lord wants us to be as healthy and whole as we can be. I have read the gospels over and over again and never saw Jesus turn down anyone who came to him for healing. The God who came down to us in and through Jesus is on the side of health. The gospels tell us of a woman who had a problem of hemorrhaging for twelve years and was embarrassed to come to Jesus openly because everyone considered her unclean. Finally, she was so desperate she decided to come up behind him in the midst of a great crowd and touch his garments. When she mustered up her courage and actually did it she was immediately healed! The historical record says the Jesus turned and said to her, "Daughter, your faith has made you well; go in peace, and be healed of your disease" (Mark 5:21-34; Luke 8:42b-48).

The Spirit of Jesus remains among us and brings healing power to us through the great channels of *nutrition* and *exercise* and miracles of healing occur through these channels every day.

We also want to affirm that this is an age exploding with remarkable acts of healing through the knowledge and growing expertise of *medical science and research.* As I write this, the newspapers are full of an exciting and moving medical triumph. Twin girls were born to Amy and Jesse Carlsen of Fargo, North Dakota. The problem was that they came into the world joined at the diaphragm, pancreas, and liver. They also shared a common bile duct and part of an intestine. These two little girls, Isabelle and Abbigail, were constantly facing each other and would hit each other in the face with their little fists even in the act of sleeping. After about three months, they were strong enough to be taken to the Mayo Clinic in Rochester, Minnesota, for the doctors to make an attempt to separate them. Shortly after their birth, a team of seventy people had been caring for the girls and preparing them for the separation attempt on Friday, May 12. On the day of the surgery, a team of thirty people, including eighteen surgeons, participated in the tightly orchestrated operation, with specialists rotating in and out of the operating room as needed.

One of the most difficult parts of the surgery was the separating of the livers because of the way the organs were fused and because the circulating structures inside the livers needed to be divided correctly. When the livers of the two girls were finally separated the whole medical team applauded, many with tears of joy in their eyes. The whole surgery took almost twelve hours. Dr. Randall Flick, their anesthesiologist said, "The girls did great. The credit goes to them. I think they are tough little girls."

What radiates in and through this remarkable miracle of surgery is the faith and the spirit of the parents. The father of the girls, Jesse Carlson, said when interviewed, "If any of you looked outside today, you noticed it was cloudy and rainy and the sun was nowhere to be seen. I think that's because the sun was in the operating room with our girls and this team. And today all of our prayers have been answered, and I can't thank you enough for helping our girls."

About five weeks after the surgery, the twin girls were sent back with their parents to their home in Fargo. Dr. Christopher Moir, who led the surgical team, said at the joyous time of their release: "Today that light that was in the operating room is out in the world. Abby and Belle came to us joined at the chest and abdomen, and they will leave us cradled arm-in-arm, as they go out into a life of light and wonder."

Moir went on to pay tribute not only to the team of nearly 100 people at Mayo who directly cared for the girls, but also to the team assembled by the parents who took over from here. It's a team that includes their families, their church, their Fargo community, Jesse Carlson's employer, "and the many thousands of people who have followed their lives and prayed for them."[7]

There continue to be many other miracles on the horizon through medical science and research. For example, we know that Alzheimer's disease is increasing for many of our older people and some not so old. To watch a loved one lose their memory and become another person who doesn't recognize you is a traumatic, sorrowful, living death. Yet more and more discoveries are being made through God's great channel of medical science and research.

The Knight Ridder News Service reports in the newspapers across our country that Alzheimer's disease could be prevented by plasmalogen contained in seafood like the oyster, sea urchin, and especially the sea squirt. Such exciting news of healing possibilities comes through a team of researchers at Tohoku University in Tokyo who stated, "We now know that the severe memory loss of

Alzheimer's disease is probably caused by the death of nerve cells in the brain." These Japanese researchers, who specialize in food chemistry, experimented with cell cultures and discovered that plasmalogen prevents the death of nerve cells. A company set up by the head of this group plans to market tablets containing plasmalogen as early as next year. Surely God is at work in this world helping us to discover anew his great healing power through science and research.[8]

**Climate For Healing**

We return now to the setting of the healing of the paralyzed lame man. The environment for this story is one surrounded by people on their way to the temple for the regular afternoon hour of prayer including Peter and John and the other apostles as well. The setting and climate of this miracle was the time of *prayer* and *worship*. It is in such a setting today that we can experience healing under the shadow of Simon Peter's leadership. In the historical account of the scriptures, we read that "more than ever believers were added to the Lord, great numbers of both men and women, so that they even carried out the sick into the streets, and laid them on cots and mats in order that Peter's shadow might fall on some of them as he came by" (Acts 5:14-15).

I want to affirm in this book that I am absolutely convinced that the real climate for healing for us is also in prayer and in acts of worship and praise. As a great physician once stated, "I do the surgery, but God steadies my hand, and God heals." How well I remember a seminary professor, Arnold Carlson, stressing the importance of prayer and holy communion in the visitation of the sick and some of the problems involved. "Sometimes," he said, "you need to make adjustments and accommodations for the sick." He went on to tell us that once in Duluth, Minnesota, he visited a man who was very sick and had great difficulty in swallowing. He could not tolerate any wine or grape juice, so in administering holy communion, Arnold used milk with the unleavened bread. Several days later, he was driving down a street in Duluth and noticed this man who had been so sick at a gas station filling up his car! Arnold stopped and visited with him and heard the man say,

"After your visit, a great peace came over me and I just knew that I was going to get well."

Mary E. Peterman is the name of a pastor's wife who had much to do with the development of healing services in our churches across the country. She writes in her little book on the subject of healing, "In receiving holy communion we are actually asking the Holy Spirit to involve us, as the body of Christ, in the healing of all mankind." She went on to share a story about John Sutherland Bonnell, a pastor and author of a book on healing, who once had a very extraordinary experience in administrating the sacrament. For many years, he cherished a close friendship with a physician and whenever the two of them got together they often celebrated holy communion as a rite of friendship and faith. What was interesting was that they always used three glasses — one for each participant and one for the "unseen guest."

In later years, this physician friend suffered a cerebral hemorrhage and his condition deteriorated rapidly so that he did not even recognize his friend or even his own family. Even so, Dr. Bonnell decided to visit the man and when they came together he set before them the usual three glasses, the wine, and the wafers with the hope that his doctor friend would be reminded that Christ was present now as he had always been before. As the service of holy communion was read aloud, the physician began to say, "Amen" at the proper times! Then a miraculous moment happened. Slowly recollection returned and they shared a period of rational remembrance and fellowship. A power was present that transcended even age and disease. Dr. Bonnell went on to say that it was one of the most dramatic experiences that he had ever had.[9]

As we stress the importance of prayer, praise, and worship in the healing process, the question of God's will comes into the picture. Certainly it is a difficult issue for many people. Yes, some people believe that they suffer because God wills it. Others say that God simply permits suffering or that it is just a part of the natural order of things in this old world. In praying for the sick, many Christians would end their prayers for healing with the words, "Heal us, Lord, if it is your will." One of my close pastor friends called this a kind of "escape clause" and that it suggests the possibility that the

Lord does not really want the person healed at this time. Mary Peterman writes about a pastor's wife who told about her experience saying, "I had a tumor removed and was recovering quite nicely when someone called on me and prayed that I would be healed, 'if it be God's will.' Suddenly I wondered if my caller had been told something I didn't know. It upset me so much to the point that it temporarily impaired my recovery."[10]

The setting for our prayers and worship should be the conviction that ultimately God's will is to heal. For one thing, there is no biblical record of anyone ever coming to Jesus for healing and being refused. Furthermore, when Jesus teaches us to pray, he tells us to say, "Thy will be done on earth as it is in heaven." Surely in the kingdom of heaven there is no sickness, disease, dying, or death. It is a place of joy where God wipes away all tears. The author Anne White would remind us:

> To say that God allows man freedom of will is not to say that he wills its misuse. God permits sickness, accidents, and wars, but he did not intentionally will or cause them. He has to allow man freedom of will or else there would be no true love — it would be coerced. Yet God is always working patiently within circumstances to draw us to voluntary acceptance of His love and of His higher intentional will. He uses our prayers of love and faith as instruments to bring about His ultimate will.[11]

At the same time, how much sickness, disease, suffering, and sorrow are the result of our own actions? And how much sickness and misery in life is caused by eating too much, drinking too much, sleeping too little, worrying too much, and being fearful and stressed out? During the more active days of my ministry, I remember visiting a man in his sixties who was dying from lung cancer. He was so miserable that he had to be propped up at night by pillows so he could try and catch his breath. As we talked together I said, "I'm sure sorry that you have to go through all this suffering." He immediately replied, "You know, pastor, I have been a heavy smoker all my life. I brought it on myself."

Through all the sicknesses and sufferings of life perhaps we need to pray for the ability to be full of thanks and praise knowing that our God through the presence of Jesus and through the power of the Spirit loves us with his constant and immeasurable love. Thanksgiving should be the climate of all our intercessions and prayers, even when God's answers are not always what we desire. Yes, the sick person for whom we pray may die but God's ultimate act of healing lies in our dying and living again.

Yes, behind the shadow of Simon Peter and behind your shadow and mine are the light and the power and the miraculous healing power of the Lord our God.

As we read on, we discover deceit and dishonesty in the early church that threatened the unity of the people under the shadow of Peter's leadership.

1. Robert Louis Stevenson, "My Shadow," from *A Child's Garden of Verses* (Edinburgh: The Westminster Press, 1983), p. 24.

2. George A. Buttrick, *The Interpreter's Dictionary of the Bible,* vol. 1 (New York/Nashville: Abingdon Press, 1962), pp. 371, 748.

3. William K. Hobart, *The Medical Language of St. Luke* (Dublin: Hodges, Figgis and Co., 1882), p. 34.

4. Story of Wesley Autrey from the Associated Press in the *New York Times,* January 3, 2007.

5. Lloyd J. Ogilvie, *The Communicator's Commentary* — *Acts* (Waco: Word Books, 1983), pp. 77-83; quote from p. 83.

6. *Mankato Free Press,* May, 2006. The same study was also found in the Twin City newspapers (*Minneapolis Star and Tribune* and the *St. Paul Dispatch*) on different days.

7. This story has been pieced together from several articles from the Associated Press as well as interviews on the *Tonight Show.* Quote from Dr. Christopher Moir in the *Mankato Free Press* (Mankato, Minnesota) on June 6, 2006.

8. This report came out in the Mankato and Twin City newspapers as well as in newspapers across the country from the Knight Ridder News Service.

9. Mary E. Peterman, *Healing, A Spiritual Adventure* (Philadelphia: Fortress Press, 1974), p. 38.

10. *Ibid*, p. 67.

11. Anne S. White, *Healing Adventure* (Evesham, England: Arthur James, 1969), pp. 29-30.

# Reflection And Discussion

## Thought Questions

1. What are the channels of God's healing in your life?

2. What are the gifts of the Holy Spirit that make us more alive than ever?

3. What is the most difficult persecution you have experienced due to your faith?

4. How does the lame man show that he is completely healed and now very courageous?


## Agree Or Disagree

• There are very few healing miracles today.

• Most people are naturally courageous.

• It is not possible to be courageous and act with boldness if you are afraid.

• Our faith would be stronger if we were persecuted more.

# Loyalty
# Under The Shadow

*Now the whole group of those who believed were of one heart and soul, and no one claimed private ownership of any possessions, but everything they owned was held in common. With great power the apostles gave their testimony to the resurrection of the Lord Jesus, and great grace was upon them all. There was not a needy person among them, for as many as owned lands or houses sold them and brought the proceeds of what was sold. They laid it at the apostles' feet, and it was distributed to each as any had need. There was a Levite, a native of Cyprus, Joseph, to whom the apostles gave the name Barnabas (which means "son of encouragement"). He sold a field that belonged to him, then brought the money, and laid it at the apostles' feet.*

— Acts 4:32-37

*But a man named Ananias, with the consent of his wife Sapphira, sold a piece of property; with his wife's knowledge, he kept back some of the proceeds, and brought only a part and laid it at the apostles' feet. "Ananias," Peter asked, "why has Satan filled your heart to lie to the Holy Spirit and to keep back part of the proceeds of the land? While it remained unsold, did it not remain your own? And after it was sold, were not the proceeds at your disposal? How is it that you have contrived this deed in your heart? You did not lie to us but to God!" Now when Ananias heard these words, he fell down and died. And great fear seized all who heard of it. The young men came and wrapped up his body, then carried him out and buried him.*

*After an interval of about three hours his wife came in, not knowing what had happened. Peter said to her, "Tell me whether you and your husband sold the land for such and such a price." And she said, "Yes, that was the price." Then Peter said to her, "How is it that you have agreed together to put the Spirit of the Lord to the test? Look, the feet of those who have buried your husband are at the door, and they will carry you out." Immediately she fell down at his feet and died. When the young men came in they found her dead, so they carried her out and buried her beside her husband. And great fear seized the whole church and all who heard of these things.* — Acts 5:1-11

*What is desirable in a person is loyalty,*
*and it is better to be poor than a liar.*
— Proverbs 19:22

If any home, family, community, or congregation is to be strong and effective there must be a loyalty to one another. Such loyalty casts a great shadow of influence upon our lives that causes us to share a caring, empowering, and nurturing force that produces great accomplishments of health, healing, and wholeness in our lives through the power of the Holy Spirit. The early church, under the shadow of the leadership of Simon Peter, not only longed for this to happen, they also made it happen.

Yes, shadows are an important part of our lives and permeate literature and stories of all kinds. In Roger Zelazny's novel, *Jack of Shadows*, the main character has a unique ability to manipulate shadows magically. In *The Lord of the Rings* by J.R.R. Tolkien, Mordor is the "land where shadows lie." Many of you who are reading this will remember that in *Peter Pan*, the main character loses his shadow. It snaps off when he leaps out the window, which is slammed down behind him. It is put in a drawer and later sewed back on by Wendy.

In history, the shadow of Simon Peter and the great shadow of the Lord our God doesn't snap off but remains upon our lives. In the prayers and praises of the psalms, the writer often speaks of living in and under the shadow of our God. In fact, the psalmist writes, "How precious is your steadfast love, O God! All people take refuge in the shadow of your wings ... for you have been my help and in the shadow of your wings I sing for joy" (Psalm 36:7; Psalm 63:7).

## The Ongoing Leadership Of Peter

Simon Peter's great shadow of leadership comes down through the centuries and influences our lives today. John Baumgaertner writes about visiting St. Peter's Cathedral in Rome on a sunny morning in early November. There before him was an image we have seen on the television screen and in the newspapers. There was the colonnaded square and the obelisk, the horse carts, and the statues. Gleaming in the sunlight was the great dome flanked by the Vatican palaces, the huge doors, and people everywhere. Once inside the vast and magnificent cathedral you could see the famous statue of the apostle Peter. Baumgaertner continues by saying, "No rough and tumble fisherman is pictured here. It is a bearded dignitary cast in bronze and bedecked with all the trappings of a pope including a great jeweled crown. How often I had wondered if it was really true that people came and kissed the bronze toe of the statue as they passed it, had kissed it so often, in fact, that in the course of the years from time to time it had been worn away and has had to be replaced."[1]

Looking into the lesson before us, one is amazed at the tremendous authority and leadership of those early apostles, especially Simon Peter. Following the ecstatic outpouring of the Holy Spirit, Peter is seen preaching in the street with great boldness and healing the sick. The streets were full of sick people on stretchers and others were just laying around in the hope that when Peter came by that if they were lucky his shadow would pass over them and they would be healed. Simon Peter and the other apostles were held in great awe. With rapidly increasing numbers, the early church worshiped Jesus as Lord and endeavored to show their love and loyalty not only to Jesus, but also to the apostles themselves. We note again the description of the church.

63

*Now the whole group of those who believed were of one heart and soul, and no one claimed private owner-ship of any possessions, but everything they owned was held in common. With great power the apostles gave their testimony to the resurrection of the Lord Jesus, and great grace was upon them all. There was not a needy person among them, for as many as owned lands or houses sold them and brought the proceeds of what was sold. They laid it at the apostles' feet, and it was distributed to each as they had need.* — Acts 4:32-35

There is a silly, old story I have loved through the years. It tells about a hillbilly who lived in the remote, wilderness, hill country of Kentucky. He and his wife had none of the modern conveniences and inventions of the age. One day he decided it was time to visit the big city. He was stunned and overwhelmed by all the things he saw. In a large department store, he came across a section that was selling all kinds of mirrors, some of them small, round mirrors with a handle. Never in his life had he seen a mirror so he picked one up, looked into it, and then remarked at the image staring back at him, "How about that! Here's a picture of my daddy!"

He promptly bought the picture and as he came back to the old farmstead he remembered that his wife, Lizzie, didn't like his fa-ther. So he hung the mirror up on one of the posts in the barn, and every morning before leaving for the fields, he would go into the barn and look into the mirror and was encouraged by what he thought was a picture of his dad.

Lizzie began to get suspicious of her husband's trips into the barn every morning before he went to work. One day after her husband left, she searched the barn and found the mirror hanging up on one of the posts. She, too, had never seen a mirror before so when she looked at her image in the mirror she exclaimed out loud, "So that's the ugly, old hag he's been seeing!"

### Reflections Of Jesus

Mirrors and reflections are found in the pages of holy scripture in Job 37:18; 2 Corinthians 3:18; and James 1:23. The mirrors of biblical times were nothing compared to the sophisticated mirrors of today with their spectacular clear images. In those days, if you wanted to see an image of yourself you could look into a clear, still pool of water in the sunlight, or you could see an image of yourself in a polished piece of pottery. Rich people had mirrors made out of highly burnished bronze but they were very expensive and the images were very dull and cloudy compared to the images in the mirrors of today. These mirrors were round in shape and many had handles made from ivory. When the apostle Paul speaks of love now and in the world to come he writes, "Now we see in a mirror, dimly, but then we will see face to face" (1 Corinthians 13:12).

The Bible teaches us that we are meant to be like mirrors in that we are reflections of the power of Jesus Christ in our lives by what we say and do. In the New Testament, James reminds us that we are to be a people that are doers of the word and then adds this little gem of wisdom: "For if any are hearers of the word and not doers, they are like those who look at themselves in a mirror; for they look at themselves and, on going away, immediately forget what they were like" (James 1:23-24).

Those early apostles, including Simon Peter, were looked upon as great reflections of Jesus. They were the true authorities of the church. When people became of one heart and soul with the apostles, they spontaneously gave up their claim to their private ownership of property and possessions. Their commitment to Jesus, to the apostles, and to each other could be spelled out L-O-Y-A-L-T-Y. They didn't want anyone who had special needs to go without help. These people were full of loving care to and for each other. Great congregations large and small today consist of a group of people who know each other as people and are well aware of those with special needs. They are loyal to each other and to their pastors and priests.

Another factor affected the people very deeply and we should make a note of it here. Time to them was a very precious thing because they expected that Jesus was coming back very soon. They lived enthusiastically in the midst of this great expectancy. Property, possessions, and private ownership were not that important because Jesus was coming back momentarily! How they must have scanned the heavens each day for the return of Jesus. Since he was coming soon, why not share their possessions together? If they sold their properties, why not give the monies to the apostles and the church? They wanted Jesus, when he returned, to find them taking care of each other, loving each other, and being loyal and committed to each other. I'm reminded of the words of a contemporary hymn we love to sing: "Soon and very soon we are goin' to see the king ... hallelujah, hallelujah, we're goin' to see the king."[2]

**An Outstanding Example Of Loyalty And Generosity**

Now our attention is focused upon some people who gave in different ways. One person in a good way and a couple who gave in a deceitful way. As someone has said, some people in our congregations are really good sheep and some are black sheep.

The first person is a man called Joseph who was a Levite and was a native of the island of Cyprus where there was a strong colony of Jews. The Levites were descendants of the tribe of Levi who assisted and served the priesthood in the sanctuary. We are told Joseph sold some property that he had owned for many years on the island of Cyprus, and he came with the money and "laid it at the apostles' feet." This Joseph had strong ties in Jerusalem because his father's family lived there and this would account for his presence in the city. Scholars believe that John Mark was the cousin of this Joseph and that the upper room where Jesus met with his disciples on the night before he died was John Mark's home. Many believe that this upper room also became the central meeting place of the apostles after the day of Pentecost.

Names are important in the scriptures and because this Joseph had been loyal to the apostles and was generous in his giving to the church, he was given the name of Barnabas, a name that means the "son of encouragement." Whenever we meet and see this Barnabas in the scriptures he is helping, encouraging, affirming, uplifting, and untiring in claiming the best for the needs of the people. You will remember that Barnabas became the apostle Paul's missionary companion and when young John Mark deserted Paul and Barnabas on that first missionary journey, Barnabas defended Mark. I can just hear Barnabas saying, "Now take it easy on Mark. He is young and probably very homesick for his family in Jerusalem. He is a good man who loves the Lord and if you are just patient with him, he will show his loyalty in many ways to our Lord and his church."

When the apostle Paul was imprisoned, Barnabas remained faithful to him and became a strong source of encouragement to him. Barnabas lived up to his name and the confidence people had in him. He surely was the essence of loyalty to the Lord, to his friends, and to the new believers.

As followers of Jesus our Lord we, too, need to be inspired by Barnabas. We are meant to be sources of encouragement to those who are around us. Close to you, my dear reader, is someone who needs your word of encouragement today. As someone said, "Encouragement puts courage into the heart of someone else." In the letter to the Ephesians, we find these succinct words: "Let no evil talk come out of your mouths but only what is useful for building up, as there is need, so that your words may give grace to those who hear" (Ephesians 4:29).

Such words are needed in our homes, families, and congregations today that we may become more alive under the shadow of those first apostles. During the course of my ministry, I have officiated at hundreds of weddings, most of them joyful indeed. In my counseling and working with couples, I would affirm with them what I would consider to be some of the important rules for a happy marriage. Here are a few of them:

- Worship and pray together.
- Communicate, communicate, communicate — to each other — every day.
- Don't be afraid of the argument and fight.
- Fight fairly by sticking to the issue at hand.
- Don't bring up the "garbage" from the past.
- Don't yell at each other unless there is a fire in the house.
- Don't let the sun set on any anger (Ephesians 4:26).
- Go to bed at peace so that morning light might find you still in love.

- Give each other a word of encouragement every day.
- Give each other a compliment every day.
- There are six little words that should be said often: "I am sorry, I was wrong!"

We return to our discourse on Barnabas. Yes, he was a good sheep in the fellowship of the early church. Yes, this Barnabas is remembered in the church today. In our church, June 11 is set aside to remember Saint Barnabas, the apostle, and the example of his giving and encouragement that comes down to us today. It is interesting to note that the special prayer for Saint Barnabas Day is as follows:

> *Grant, almighty God, that we may follow the example of your faithful servant, Barnabas, who, seeking not his own renown but the well-being of your church, gave generously of his life and substance for the relief of the poor and the spread of the gospel, through Jesus Christ our Lord, who lives and reigns with you and the Holy Spirit, one God, now and forever. Amen.*[3]

**Examples Of Dishonesty And Disloyalty**

We must turn to the story of Ananias and Sapphira who are looked upon as the black sheep of the early church. Is it not true that in our congregations all people are sinners and in need of forgiveness? We say in the Apostles' Creed that we believe in "the holy catholic church, the communion of saints" indicating that we are all saints and sinners but please note here that "saints" has a small "s." Someone has said that the church might be a "communion of saints" but it is also a "hospital for hypocrites." If perfection were required for church membership today, there would be no church. We raise the question, "What was so bad about Ananias and Sapphira?" Maybe we should also raise the question, "Did Simon Peter, the great spiritual leader of the church whose shadow rests upon us, bring about the death of these people?" How well I remember a Bible study on the book of Acts in a congregation in Boone, Iowa, in which someone made the comment, "I don't like the story of Ananias and Sapphira! It makes me feel so uncomfortable!" So we take a closer look.

Names are important in the Bible and we note here that the Hebrew form of the name "Ananias" means "God is gracious" and the name "Sapphira" means "beautiful." There is nothing gracious about what Ananias did, nor anything beautiful about Sapphira's collusive cooperation with her husband in their pretense of loyalty to the Lord and the early church. The greatness of that church was the loyalty of the people to the Lord and their loyalty to each other. These people wanted no one to be in need. They shared all they could so that no one would be lacking in care and love. If the members had property and wealth, they were free to keep it for themselves and if they sold their property and goods, they were not forced to bring it to the apostles for the common good.

The problem with Ananias and Sapphira was that they *pretended* to give *all* of the proceeds of the sale of their property to the church. They had promised the leaders of the church that all of their monies would be given. Yet, they decided to secretly keep back a portion of the monies for their own desires. If there were extraordinary circumstances or needs in their lives, they could have told Peter and the other apostles openly about their needs and wants. The problem is that they withheld some of their proceeds secretly so they could receive the honor, praise, and recognition from the whole church. Many scholars point out that this was a form of embezzlement!

Simon Peter was gifted with spiritual discernment and could read their hearts and minds. It was written on their faces. Their grand announcements about giving all they had were a cover-up for their lying and deceit that had occurred over a period of time. This dishonesty was undermining not only their loyalty to the church, but it became a temptation to other members to withhold some of their giving secretly as well. Lloyd Ogilvie goes so far as to say:

> *We can't lie to God. He knows everything anyhow. The dangerous thing is pretending with the fellowship of believers. God is never deceived. His heart breaks over what we do with the gift of life, but we can't fool him.*

*Because he has given us freedom, we can block his best*
*for us. The dishonesty of duality spreads like cancer.*
*When we are not real and authentic with others, it is*
*difficult for them to be genuine with us. Spiritual su-*
*perficiality sets in. The great holdout becomes a hold-*
*up.*[4]

When Ananias is confronted with his dishonesty and secrecy, the sense of his own guilt fell upon him like a terrible shock and the stress of it all was enough to kill him. Three hours later, when Sapphira was confronted she, too, must have felt the guilt and stress of it all. When she heard of the sudden death of her husband, the stress and shock of it all killed her, too. To us today, it can seem like a cruel kind of fate. Surely it offends our sense of tolerance that we have cultivated in the church today. To some people, the deaths of Ananias and Sapphira seem to deny the mercy of God and to violate the spirit of lovingkindness that Jesus displayed. To Jesus, one of the greatest of sins was hypocrisy and dishonesty. One day, Jesus lashed out at the hypocrisy of the Pharisees by saying: "Woe to you, scribes and Pharisees, hypocrites! For you are like whitewashed tombs, which on the outside look beautiful, but inside they are full of the bones of the dead and of all kinds of filth. So you also on the outside look righteous to others, but inside you are full of hypocrisy and lawlessness" (Matthew 23:27-28).

Strong words from Jesus, but he knew that dishonesty and hypocrisy can destroy a person and be like a leprosy spreading throughout the community of his followers. At the same time, Jesus was unbelievably merciful to those who were genuinely repentant over their weaknesses.

**The Energizing Force Of Loyalty**
Loyalty to one another and a genuineness of concern for each other can be a powerful energizing force in today's world, enabling us to be a people more alive than ever. You and I have seen athletic teams whose personnel and coaches possessed such loyalty and caring concern for each other that it created a team spirit that enabled them to play the game way beyond their talents and abilities.

Take the case of Jason McElwain who has been autistic since he was very young.

Based on the statistics from the United States Department of Education, autism, a disease that affects an individual's ability to relate socially to others, is growing at a rate of 10% to 17% a year, making it the fastest growing disability in the country. The disease cuts across all racial, ethnic, social, and economic lines, yet it affects boys four times more often than girls ... and there is no known cure.

When most people think of autism, their minds immediately think of Raymond Babbitt, Dustin Hoffman's character in the film *Rain Man*. But the disease is far more complex than that, imposing wide-ranging effects on its subjects. Some are left speechless or entirely unable to communicate, while others face miniature hurdles each day that often aren't readily visible to those on the outside.

When Jason McElwain, though autistic, became a high school student at the Greece Athena High School in Rochester, New York, he found a community of students who accepted him totally. Everyone called him J-MAC and teachers and coaches worked hard to make him feel at home. By the time he was a senior, the basketball coach and team members made him the student manager of the basketball team.

Then something happened to the coach and the team. They fell in love with J-MAC and he with them. They were loyal to him and tried to help him in every way, even letting him shoot baskets before and after the practice sessions. Though he was autistic he became quite a shooter, especially with long distance shots. As the season drew to a close, Coach Jim Johnson added J-MAC to the roster of the team so he could be given a jersey and be able to sit on the bench in the team's last game of the year. Johnson hoped the situation would even enable him to get McElwain onto the floor for a little playing time since it was also "senior night." J-MAC sat patiently on the bench in his new uniform until the team was up twenty points. His fellow students were chanting his name and the coach put him in the game with four minutes to go.

In his first action of the year, McElwain missed his first two shots, "My first shot was an air ball (missing the hoop), by a lot,

71

then I missed a lay-up," McElwain recalls. Then something happened. With the crowd chanting his name, he suddenly caught fire. He went on to sink six three-pointers and then another shot for a total of twenty points in three minutes. Saying that the crowd went wild is an understatement. They chanted his name over and over again and each basket was followed by a roar as if he had just won the game in the final second with each shot. Maybe he did because the game of life was being won because of the intense loyalty and love that permeated the crowd.

"A lot of us feel like this is our gift to have this happen and to have it receive so much nationwide publicity," said Dr. Catherine Lord, a professor of psychiatry and the director for the University of Michigan's Autism and Communications Disorders Center. "There are thousands of Jasons out there carrying the net for the soccer team, keeping statistics for the basketball team, and playing the drum for the school band. This serves as a reminder to give these kids a chance whenever possible."[5]

The early Christian church was like a team — loyal to each other, and to their coach, Jesus Christ. They genuinely cared for each other and wanted all cares, needs, and sicknesses ministered to and healed. They shared all things in common and possessed an immeasurable spirit of oneness. Under the shadow of the leadership of Simon Peter, everything was done to keep the young church united and strong and cheering and chanting for each other, accomplishing acts of faith that were beyond understanding. Anything that smacked of disloyalty, dishonesty, selfishness, and greed was weeded out by the power of the Spirit.

Yes, if any home or family, community or congregation is to be strong and effective, there must be loyalty to one another. Simon Peter needed to face the greatest decision of his life. His decision would determine dramatically the future course of the young church.

---

1. John Baumgaertner, *Meet the Twelve* (Minneapolis: Augsburg Publishing House, 1960), pp. 112-113. This book is a series of sermons on the original twelve disciples that is well illustrated and quoted from through the years.

2. "Soon And Very Soon," Hymn 744, *With One Voice* (Minneapolis: Augsburg Fortress, 1995), text and music by Andraé Crouch, copyright 1976. Copyright held by EMI music in Nashville.

3. "St. Barnabas, Apostle," *Lutheran Book of Worship* (Minneapolis: Augsburg Publishing House and Philadelphia: Board of Publication, Lutheran Church in America, 1978), p. 33.

4. Lloyd J. Ogilvie, *The Communicator's Commentary — Acts* (Waco: Word Books, 1983), p. 110.

5. This story was pieced together from numerous news reports. A special thank you to Pastor Don Thompson of the Love of Christ Church in Mesa, Arizona, who preached a sermon centered on the story of Jason McElwain.

# Reflection And Discussion

**Thought Questions**

1. Why did those early Christians sell everything and share with those in need?

2. What was so good about this Joseph in our story?

3. What was so bad about Ananias and Sapphira?

4. What does this story say about the authenticity of the scriptures?

**Agree Or Disagree**

• Peter was responsible for the deaths of Ananias and Sapphira.

• Peter shows great leadership skills in this story.

• The story of Ananias and Sapphira makes us feel good about ourselves.

• Money is the root of all evil (1 Timothy 6:10).

• This story denies the mercy of God.

# Acceptance Under The Shadow

## Part 1

Peter and Cornelius

*In Caesarea there was a man named Cornelius, a centurion of the Italian Cohort, as it was called. He was a devout man who feared God with all his household; he gave alms generously to the people and prayed constantly to God. One afternoon at about three o'clock he had a vision in which he clearly saw an angel of God coming in and saying to him, "Cornelius." He stared at him in terror and said, "What is it, Lord?" He answered, "Your prayers and your alms have ascended as a memorial before God. Now send men to Joppa for a certain Simon who is called Peter; he is lodging with Simon, a tanner, whose house is by the seaside." When the angel who spoke to him had left, he called two of his slaves and a devout soldier from the ranks of those who served him, and after telling them everything, he sent them to Joppa.*

*About noon the next day, as they were on their journey and approaching the city, Peter went up on the roof to pray. He became hungry and wanted something to eat; and while it was being prepared, he fell into a trance. He saw the heaven opened and something like a large sheet coming down, being lowered to the ground by its four corners. In it were all kinds of four-footed creatures and reptiles and birds of the air. Then he heard a voice saying, "Get up, Peter; kill and eat." But Peter said, "By no means, Lord; for I have never eaten anything that is profane and unclean." The voice said to him again, a second time, "What God has made clean, you must not call profane." This happened three times, and the thing was suddenly taken up to heaven.*

*Now while Peter was greatly puzzled about what to make of the vision that he had seen, suddenly the men sent by Cornelius appeared. They were asking for Simon's house and were standing by the gate. They called out to ask whether Simon, who was called Peter, was staying there. While Peter was still thinking about the vision, the Spirit said to him, "Look, three men are searching for you. Now get up, go down, and go with them without hesitation; for I have sent them." So Peter went down to the men and said, "I am the one you are looking for; what is the reason for your coming?" They answered, "Cornelius, a centurion, an upright and God-fearing man, who is well spoken of by the whole Jewish nation, was directed by a holy angel to send for you to come to his house and to hear what you have to say." So Peter invited them in and gave them lodging.*

— Acts 10:1-23a

## Part 2

*The next day he got up and went with them, and some of the believers from Joppa accompanied him. The following day they came to Caesarea. Cornelius was expecting them and had called together his relatives and close friends. On Peter's arrival Cornelius met him, and falling at his feet, worshiped him. But Peter made him get up, saying, "Stand up; I am only a mortal." And as he talked with him, he went in and found that many had assembled; and he said to them, "You yourselves know that it is unlawful for a Jew to associate with or to visit a Gentile; but God has shown me that I should not call anyone profane or unclean. So when I was sent for, I came without objection. Now may I ask why you sent for me?"*

*Cornelius replied, "Four days ago at this very hour, at three o'clock, I was praying in my house when suddenly a man in dazzling clothes stood before me. He said, 'Cornelius, your prayer has been heard and your alms have been remembered before God. Send therefore to Joppa and ask for Simon, who is called Peter; he is staying in the home of Simon, a tanner, by the sea.' Therefore I sent for you immediately, and you have been kind enough to come. So now all of us are here in the presence of God to listen to all that the Lord has commanded you to say."*

Gentiles Hear The Good News

*Then Peter began to speak to them: "I truly understand that God shows no partiality, but in every nation anyone who fears him and does what is right is acceptable to him. You know the message he sent to the people of Israel, preaching peace by Jesus Christ — he is Lord of all. That message spread throughout Judea, beginning in Galilee after the baptism that John announced: how God anointed Jesus of Nazareth with the Holy Spirit and with power; how he went about doing good and healing all who were oppressed by the devil, for God was with him. We are witnesses to all that he did both in Judea and in Jerusalem. They put him to death by hanging him on a tree; but God raised him on the third day and allowed him to appear, not to all the people but to us who were chosen by God as witnesses, and who ate and drank with him after he rose from the dead. He commanded us to preach to the people and to testify that he is the one ordained by God as judge of the living and the dead. All the prophets testify about him that everyone who believes in him receives forgiveness of sins through his name."*

Gentiles Receive The Holy Spirit

*While Peter was still speaking, the Holy Spirit fell upon all who heard the word. The circumcised believers who had come with Peter were astounded that the gift of the Holy Spirit had been poured out even on the Gentiles, for they heard them speaking in tongues and extolling God. Then Peter said, "Can anyone withhold the water for baptizing these people who have received the Holy Spirit just as we have?" So he ordered them to be baptized in the name of Jesus Christ. Then they invited him to stay for several days.* — Acts 10:23b-48

77

*Whoever loves a brother or sister lives in the light,*
*and in such a person there is no cause for stumbling.*
— 1 John 2:10

## Part 1

In the midst of all his afflictions and miseries, Job felt despondent and alone. He cried out in his despair, saying, "A mortal, born of woman, few of days and full of trouble, comes up like a flower and withers, flees like a shadow and does not last" (Job 14:1-2). Yet Job would also experience finally the restoration of health and wealth and would know the comfort of God's acceptance like a cool shadow on his days. All of us can pray with the psalmist: "Guard me as the apple of the eye; hide me in the shadow of your wings ..." (Psalm 17:8). It is this comfort of the shadow of God upon our lives that enables us to be more alive than ever.

Shadows are indeed a part of our lives and reach out even into the space around us. We know that a shadow cast by earth on the moon is a lunar eclipse. Conversely, a shadow cast by the moon onto earth is a solar eclipse. In photographs taken from satellites, tall buildings can be recognized by their long shadows, as long as the photographs are not taken in the tropics around noon. We affirm again that the shadow of Simon Peter is a long and immeasurable one through the centuries influencing us and our faith. This shadow of influence can change our directions of life and enable us to become really alive. Simon Peter helps us to realize as never before the great love and acceptance that God has for us, an acceptance that we can share with those around us.

### Acceptance In The Church

As we look again upon the life of Peter, we discover that he has a growing problem concerning which people should be accepted into the fellowship of the early Christian church. This is a problem that comes down to us today, for often the church struggles with what kind of people should be acceptable into the membership and fellowship. In serving as an interim pastor of a large church in downtown Des Moines, I became acquainted with a man who had HIV/AIDS and who had found it difficult to be accepted in some of the congregations because of the stigma associated with his disease. He was an excellent teacher, but some of the congregations would not accept him in such a position.

Finally, he found a place in our congregation and was immediately accepted as a teacher of youth. In this role, he was a guest one Wednesday evening at our eighth-grade confirmation class. He spoke of his AIDS and how he had contracted the disease through contaminated blood transfusions. He went on to describe his daily weaknesses and fevers along with all kinds of aches and pains. Opening up a black case, he displayed all the pills (dozens of them) that he had to take each day and the resulting nausea and weaknesses with which he battled and that, at times, made it difficult for him to function. Then he made a stirring witness to his faith in our Lord that sustained him each day. Some of the students and their parents who were present left with tears in their eyes including myself. Yes, not only was this man lifted up by his faith, but also by the welcome and acceptance he found in the congregation.

Simon Peter's dilemma was what should be done with the Gentiles. Should the new young church accept them or not, and if they were accepted, would their confession of faith and baptism be enough? Many of the conservative leaders believed that Gentiles needed to be circumcised and carefully instructed in Judaism, that is to say, they needed to be Jews first and then become a part of the church. We know that Peter was wrestling with the problem and was in the process of arriving at a whole new conviction. A change of attitude toward those who are different requires often a long and hard struggle. When we catch up with Peter in this lesson we discover that he is living with a person that many looked down upon and considered unclean. He was known as Simon the tanner, which meant that he had to work with dead animals. An orthodox Jew was not permitted to have dealings with anyone who worked with such things, because it made them unclean. That's the reason tanners had to live fifty cubits outside a village, and in the case of Simon the tanner not only outside the village of Joppa but right on the shores of the Mediterranean Sea.[1]

This tanner outside of Joppa was helpful to Peter because he was a believer in Jesus, and Peter found in him a friend, in spite of all the rules and regulations. In those days, a strict Jew believed that the one true God had no use for the Gentiles and that God's message and favor extended to the Jews and Jews alone. They looked down upon these dirty Gentiles and believed that no help should be given even to a Gentile woman in childbirth.[2] The heart of Peter was softening and he was on his way to a whole new outlook that would give him a new kind of freedom and abundant life. The revelation of God through the coming of Jesus Christ was not meant for the Jews alone but for the whole world!

## The Hurt Of Unacceptance

Sometimes the problem and hurt of not being accepted can be experienced at an early age. As a boy in the second grade, I remember wearing a tan sport coat to school. My grandmother, with whom I lived, had dry cleaned it with some kind of kerosene solution and obviously the coat must have reeked with a strong odor that I had become used to and didn't even notice. The other children began to complain to the teacher about the odor in the classroom and soon she went up and down the rows smelling each child's clothing. Imagine my embarrassment when she made me stand up and walk out of the classroom with her. She took my little sport coat off and hung it on an outside door. There was a lot of snickering when I returned to the classroom with just my T-shirt and no sport coat. No question about it, I felt ridiculed and not accepted. Before the day was over, during the recess period, my classmates began to show me that it didn't make any difference to them if I had a smelly coat — even though it gave them a big laugh. I learned early on that a climate of not being accepted, even if imagined, was painful indeed.

## A Soldier Called Cornelius

Our attention is focused upon a Roman soldier by the name of Cornelius. His story marks a turning point in the history of the church when it came to accepting Gentiles, in fact, Cornelius and his family and friends were the first Gentile members.

Cornelius was an officer known as a centurion who was stationed in Caesarea where the headquarters of the Roman government of Palestine was located. At this point, it is helpful to notice how the Roman military was organized. First of all, there were legions consisting of 1,000 men each. Each legion was divided into ten cohorts having 600 men each, and each cohort was divided into six centuries having 100 men. Cornelius, as a centurion, was in charge of 100 men and as such an officer had a reputation for being brave and courageous. Such officers were chosen carefully and were trained to take great caution and care before going on the offensive. They were steady individuals who were prudent in their actions and commands. If in a battle they were overwhelmed and hard-pressed, they would stand fast and be willing to die for their country.[3] Jesus himself was well aware of how the Roman army was organized. When Peter tried to defend Jesus in the Garden of Gethsemane he told him to put away his sword and said, "Do you think that I cannot appeal to my Father, and he will at once send me more than twelve legions of angels?" (Matthew 26:55). Wow! More than 72,000 defending Jesus would have been quite a sight!

Cornelius was much more than just an ordinary brave Roman officer. We are told that he was a "devout man who feared God with all his household" and that "he gave alms generously and prayed constantly to God" (Acts 10:2). Somewhere along the line he had been attracted to the religion of the Jews and had embraced the monotheism of the Hebrew faith. He was searching with all of his heart for meaning and understanding. As a Gentile, his growing faith in the one true God inspired him to great acts of charity. He became known as a man of prayer and was loved by the Jewish people who had come to know him. It is this Roman soldier, this well-loved man, who would enable Peter to change and become a person of great tolerance and acceptance.

All of us have had people in our lives that by their actions and words have influenced us and caused us to change directions in life. I remember a Sunday school teacher, a man of great faith, who influenced me in many ways. It wasn't just what he said, but it was also his actions and his sense of reverence. How carefully he would hold the Bible when he read it and how beautifully he would say small, spontaneous prayers. Often when he told a story of Jesus, I was amazed at the emotion and drama he would put into the telling. Since I didn't have a father and was being raised by my grandmother, he became the father I never had. He let me work in his small grocery store in Fargo, North Dakota. I looked forward to the Saturday lunches in his home and to the times he would take me to his small farm along the Red River. He would take me to the annual father and son banquet at Olivet Church and I was so proud to pretend to be his son. His kindness and generosity turned my life around and, even though I was only nine years old, I began to think about the possibilities of serving others in the church. So it was with Cornelius. His kindness and generosity as a Roman officer and his great acts of charity as a Gentile would attract the attention of Peter, as well as the Jews of the whole area, and turn Peter's life in another direction. Nevertheless, such a change in Peter would require divine intervention.

### The Visions Of Peter And Cornelius

One day at the home of Simon the tanner, during the noon hour, Peter went up on the flat roof to pray. There he could see a spectacular view of the Mediterranean with its sparkling blue waters and the sails of the passing ships and he could hear the crashing of the waves against the shore. He felt very hungry and was looking forward to the meal that was being prepared below. Suddenly, he fell into a trance and saw a large sheet coming down out of the sky containing all kinds of four-footed animals along with reptiles and birds. Then he heard a vibrant voice saying to him, "Get up, Peter; kill and eat." The Jewish people had very strict food laws (see Leviticus 11 and Deuteronomy 14:1-21) that governed what was clean and unclean. Only animals that had divided hoofs and chewed the cud were acceptable for eating. For example, the pig was considered unclean and not acceptable because even though it had divided hoofs, it didn't chew the cud. No animals of the sea could be eaten except those with fins and scales. The only insects that were acceptable were those with jointed legs that could jump, for example the locusts, grasshoppers, and crickets. I remember an old cartoon that showed John the Baptist as a young boy with his mother. In the caption under the cartoon, the mother was pictured as saying to her son, "If you aren't a good boy and do your chores, you cannot eat your locusts and honey!" When Peter saw the vision and was told to kill and eat, he felt nothing but revulsion and exclaimed that he had never eaten anything unclean. Three times Peter was told to kill and eat (I suppose for extra emphasis). God himself was teaching Peter a lesson. Suddenly the vision was ended and we are told that Peter was "greatly puzzled." The Greek word here implies wonderment along with being deeply perplexed and distressed — but not for long.[4] Suddenly, Peter heard a commotion and heard his name being called from the outer gate.

While all this was going on, something else had been happening that would be changing the course of Cornelius. The day before Peter had his vision, an angel appeared to Cornelius about 3:00 in the afternoon and in his terror and fear he heard the angel tell him that his prayers had been heard. He was told his giving had been noticed and that he was to send messengers to Joppa to bring back Peter, who was staying at the home of Simon the tanner. Cornelius sent two of his slaves and a devout soldier to seek out Peter and to bring him back to Cornelius' home in Caesarea, about forty miles north of Joppa where Peter lived. It took them until the next day to come to where Peter was staying and it was those men who were calling for Peter at the outer gate, all of them Gentiles. The miracle of the moment is that when Peter came out of his trance and vision and found out who it was that knocked and shouted at the outer gate, even though they were Gentiles, he welcomed them into the place where he was staying and they spent the night together! That was unheard of — Gentiles living, breathing, eating, conversing, and sleeping under the same roof as Peter! Nothing would ever be the same again. Peter's shadow of influence was expanding. His spirit of acceptance was being nourished and developed. The earthquake was beginning and the rock of Peter was splitting at the epicenter.

What are the forces that cause you and me to turn in another direction and in the process become more alive than ever?

Oftentimes it is not a big vision, but rather a gentle suggestion from a good friend or a series of coincidences that changes one's heart and mind. We can be influenced by a movie, play, or a piece of music that touches the heart. It can happen because of serious sickness and a return of health. Once when I was making hospital rounds I visited a man who had been in the hospital for some time and when I asked him how he was doing he replied, "Well, pastor, at least being in bed all this time has caused me to look up and I don't mean just at the ceiling!"

There is a silly, old story I want to share here because it did change the direction of a marriage. A husband and wife were having a breakfast together before the husband was going to work. Suddenly in their conversation she said to him, "I bet you don't even know what day this is!" On his way to work, the husband was disturbed. What special day had he forgotten? Was it an anniversary or some other special day? Perhaps it was the birthday of someone in her family. At 10:00 that morning the doorbell rang and the wife ran to the door. She was handed a dozen long-stem beautiful red roses. At 1:00 in the afternoon, a beautiful foil-wrapped, two-pound box of her favorite chocolates was delivered, and then at 4 p.m., the local boutique delivered an exquisite designer dress that fit her perfectly. That evening she greeted her husband coming home from work with the words: "What a great day! This is the best and most wonderful Groundhog's Day I have ever experienced!" From that day on, the husband made it a special point in their lives to remember the really important days!

## Part 2
### A New Beginning
The morning after Peter spent the night with the Gentile messengers was really a new beginning for Peter. With excitement, he went with them back to Caesarea to the home of Cornelius. They were also joined on this journey by some of the believers from Joppa. These six other people[5] were legalistic Jews who were going to watch what Peter would do with the Gentiles very carefully. They were part of the legalistic conservative group of Hebrew Christians who believed that the only way to become a part of the

new young Christian church was through full participation in Judaism, including all the rites and rituals of Israel, including circumcision. The journey up the coast to Caesarea certainly gave Peter some meditative time to become prepared to face Cornelius and his family along with their searching questions.

As we have learned, Caesarea was the Roman government center of operations for the area. I have vivid memories of visiting the city and its ruins. You can still see the huge rocks that were piled up and secured in the sea to form a wall of shelter against the blustery waves and thus a well-protected harbor for the ships of that time. How they were moved and shaped and formed in the sea is beyond one's imagination in an age of no big machinery and equipment. What a beautiful sight it was to see the great expanse of the blue Mediterranean stretching out to the far horizon. The crashing of the waves against the shore seemed to be a voice shouting, "Peter was here and in this beautiful setting he was shaped and formed into a new, dynamic man who learned what it meant to be accepting toward the Gentiles." Among the ruins, but still standing, was the ancient aqueduct that stretched off into the distant hills and had been the conduit of running water for the city. We also were led to the ruins of a great amphitheater that still looked in good enough condition for the production of plays. Those ancient people must have known something about the principles of acoustics in the building of amphitheaters. Two members of our group stood in the center of the round stage area while the rest of us sat in the top row. Even when the people on the stage talked in a whisper we could still hear them distinctly. And something else — even though the sun was high in the sky, the shadow of Peter and his words of acceptance to the Gentiles were felt and heard.

### Peter And Cornelius — Acceptance And New Life

When Peter and his entourage arrived at the home of Cornelius, they discovered that Cornelius was not alone, for he had gathered together not only his family, but many of his friends as well! A great step now is taken when Peter is invited in and crosses the threshold into the home where all these Gentiles are gathered.

Cornelius himself is overwhelmed and kneels before Peter to honor and worship him. But Peter would have nothing to do with this and tells Cornelius to stand up since they were both mortals. Peter is quite diplomatic in his approach in that he acknowledges Jews were taught to have no dealings with Gentiles but that something has happened. God has shown him that he is not to look down upon or call anyone profane or unclean. Then he very graciously asks them why they have invited him. Cornelius recounts his vision of the angel who commanded him to send for Peter and thanks him for his willingness to come and assures him that they are most willing to hear what the Lord wants to say through him.

What follows is the good news of the coming of Jesus. I am most certain that these words of Peter are just a summary of his teaching concerning the Christian faith, but it is enough to catch the flavor of the proceedings. Peter shares with them the story of Jesus as the one promised through the ages and through the message of the prophets. Jesus was sent by a great God of love and equipped with the Spirit's power to bring a ministry of healing and forgiveness and then was crucified and on the third day of his death he was resurrected and now lives! Through this living Jesus there is given the message of a new abundant life and a new relationship with a loving God that is meant for everyone. No wonder Peter begins his teaching with words that echo through the centuries and are often quoted today: "I truly understand that God shows no partiality, but in every nation anyone who fears him and does what is right is acceptable to him" (Acts 10:34-35).

Something happened to the group that convinced Peter more than ever that Gentiles were to be received into the fellowship of the Christian church. We read that "while Peter was still speaking, the Holy Spirit fell upon all who heard the word." And how did Peter know that this had happened? There occurred in that moment a phenomenon known as speaking in tongues that happened often in the early church. Even those six "circumcised believers" who had come with Peter were amazed that such a gift was given to the Gentiles. I just bet those six people left quickly by the side door to rush to Jerusalem to let the leaders know what was happening to

Peter and his relationship to the Gentiles! In this wondrous moment of joy and thanksgiving, Peter ordered the whole group to be baptized and a new age of the church had begun (Acts 10:44-48).

Speaking in tongues, as many of you who are reading this can verify, is a result of being so filled with emotion and ecstasy in the faith that words just babble forth that cannot be controlled and cannot be understood unless there is an interpreter on hand. Everyone with whom I have spoken who has experienced this phenomenon speaks of how much their faith has deepened. I have spoken with many of our missionaries who state that it is a common experience in the development of our churches in Africa. They describe the experience as a power surge within a person of thanksgiving and joy and that the babbling of words though not always understood are words full of praise to God.

Speaking in tongues was certainly one of the gifts of the Spirit in the early Christian church of the first century and, after being dormant for a time, emerged again in the last century and on into this one. In Cedar Falls, Iowa, some years ago a healing service was held in the domed athletic stadium on the campus of the University of Northern Iowa on a Sunday afternoon under the direction of a Roman Catholic priest known as Father Diorio. The stadium was filled with thousands of people including a Catholic couple who were our very good friends and had invited us to be with them. The wife had a cancerous tumor that was malignant in one of her lungs and she felt that such a healing service could do nothing but help. There was a great choir with wondrous music and the priest sitting behind the choir gave short messages of healing from the scriptures.

Spontaneously, the huge throng of people began to sing choruses together and I began to feel the power of the Spirit among us. There was an outbreak of speaking in tongues that startled me and it was helpful to me to know that these emotions of ecstasy were really words of praise and joy. The service lasted about four hours and when I had to leave early because of a meeting, it was with great reluctance. Some time later we found out that our friend's wife had a physical exam and, to the astonishment of the doctors, the cancerous tumor was gone. Today, many years later, she is still alive.

I have had many vibrant emotional experiences of worship but have not experienced speaking in tongues. I find the words of the apostle Paul in his first letter to the Corinthian Christians very helpful. Paul obviously had experienced the phenomenon of speaking in tongues himself and it was certainly found in the missionary congregations that he established. He often listed the gifts of the Spirit in the order of their importance but always listed speaking in tongues last and was convinced that if speaking in tongues were present in the worship there should be an interpreter. In his first letter to the church at Corinth he wrote: "I thank God that I speak in tongues more than all of you; nevertheless, in church I would rather speak five words with my mind, in order to instruct others also, than ten thousand words in a tongue" (1 Corinthians 14:18). A fellow pastor said to me that the gift of tongues is offered to all Christians but is required of none — but to be honest I will always remain open to the experience.

As we return to the Cornelius story, we want to note here that the water baptism that followed the pouring out of the Spirit must have been the most joyful and moving of experiences. Here was a pronouncement of the fact without any reservation that Gentiles were welcome into the fellowship of the church. Because of the shadow of influence of Peter and the outpouring of the Spirit, the church moved into a new direction of acceptance.

## Acceptance In Our Lives And The Church Today

Acceptance remains a problem in the fellowship of the church. Are everyone and anyone acceptable to us if they believe in Jesus as Lord and Savior and make a commitment to follow him? What about illegal immigrants, people with AIDS, or those who are physically or mentally handicapped? What about people of different color and different accents and different styles of life? What about gays and lesbians? Sometimes such a question threatens the very fabric of the church and requires much more study not only physically, mentally, spiritually, and scientifically, but also requires a serious study of the holy scripture and the social background of its pronouncements. For example, the Bible accepts slavery that we condemn today. The problem of acceptance is not only in the church, but it is found in our homes and families, as well as in our businesses and places of work today. Listen to the story from the owner of a restaurant in a truck stop.

> *I try not to be biased, but I had my doubts about hiring Stevie. His placement counselor assured me that he would be a good, reliable busboy. But I had never had a mentally handicapped employee and wasn't sure I wanted one. I wasn't sure how my customers would react to Stevie.*
>
> *He was short, a little dumpy with the smooth facial features and thick-tongued speech of Down syndrome. I wasn't worried about most of my trucker customers because truckers don't generally care who buses tables as long as the meatloaf platter is good and the pies are homemade.*
>
> *The four-wheeler drivers were the ones who concerned me; the mouthy college kids traveling to school; the yuppie snobs who secretly polish their silverware with their napkins for fear of catching some dreaded "truck-stop germ"; the pairs of white-shirted businessmen on expense accounts who think every truck-stop waitress wants to be flirted with. I knew those people would be uncomfortable around Stevie so I closely watched him for the first few weeks.*
>
> *I shouldn't have worried. After the first week, Stevie had my staff wrapped around his stubby little finger, and within a month my truck regulars had adopted him as their official truck-stop mascot.*
>
> *After that, I really didn't care what the rest of the customers thought of him. He was like a 21-year-old in blue jeans and Nikes, eager to laugh and eager to please, but fierce in his attention to his duties. Every salt and pepper shaker was exactly in its place, not a bread crumb or coffee spill was visible when Stevie got done with the table. Our only problem was persuading him to wait to clean a table until after the customers*

*were finished. He would hover in the background, shifting his weight from one foot to the other, scanning the dining room until a table was empty. Then he would scurry to the empty table and carefully bus dishes and glasses onto his cart and meticulously wipe the table up with a practiced flourish of his rag.*

*If he thought a customer was watching, his brow would pucker with added concentration. He took pride in doing his job exactly right, and you had to love how hard he tried to please each and every person he met.*

*Over time, we learned that he lived with his mother, a widow who was disabled after repeated surgeries for cancer. They lived on their Social Security benefits in public housing two miles from the truck stop. Their social worker, who stopped to check on him every so often, admitted Stevie and his mom had fallen between the cracks. Money was tight, and what I paid him was probably the difference between them being able to live together and Stevie being sent to a group home. That's why the restaurant was a gloomy place that morning last August, the first morning in three years that Stevie missed work.*

*He was at the Mayo Clinic in Rochester getting a new valve or something put in his heart. His social worker said that people with Down syndrome often have heart problems at an early age so this wasn't unexpected, and there was a good chance he would come through the surgery in good shape and be back at work in a few months.*

*A ripple of excitement ran through the staff later that morning when word came that he was out of surgery, in recovery, and doing fine.*

*Frannie, the head waitress, let out a war whoop and did a little dance in the aisle when she heard the good news.*

*One of our regular trucker customers stared at the sight of this fifty-year-old grandmother of four doing a victory shimmy beside his table.*

*Frannie blushed, smoothed her apron, and shot the driver a withering look.*

*He grinned. "Okay, Frannie, what was that all about?" he asked.*

*"We just got word that Stevie is out of surgery and going to be okay," she replied.*

*"I was wondering where he was. I had a new joke to tell him. What was the surgery about?"*

*Frannie quickly told him and the other two drivers sitting at his booth about Stevie's surgery, then sighed: "Yeah, I'm glad he is going to be okay," she said. "But I don't know how he and his mom are going to handle all the bills. From what I hear, they're barely getting by as it is."*

*The trucker nodded thoughtfully, and Frannie hurried off to wait on the rest of her tables. Since I hadn't had time to round up a busboy to replace Stevie and really didn't want to replace him, the girls were busing their own tables that day until we decided what to do.*

The story goes on to tell that money "For Stevie" began showing up, tucked under napkins and left on plates for three months. The story continues.

*Today is Thanksgiving, the first day Stevie is supposed to be back to work.*

*His placement worker said he's been counting the days until the doctor said he could work, and it didn't matter at all that it was a holiday. He called ten times in the past week, making sure we knew he was coming, fearful that we had forgotten him or that his job was in jeopardy. I arranged to have his mother bring him to work. I then met them in the parking lot and invited them both to celebrate his day back.*

*Stevie was thinner and paler, but couldn't stop grinning as he pushed through the doors and headed for the back room where his apron and busing cart were waiting.*

*"Hold up there, Stevie, not so fast," I said. I took him and his mother by their arms. "Work can wait for a minute. To celebrate your coming back, breakfast for*

*you and your mother is on me!" I led them toward a*
*large corner booth at the rear of the room.*

    *I could feel and hear the rest of the staff following*
*behind as we marched through the dining room. Glanc-*
*ing over my shoulder, I saw booth after booth of grin-*
*ning truckers get up and join the procession. We stopped*
*in front of the big table. Its surface was covered with*
*coffee cups, saucers, and dinner plates, all sitting*
*slightly crooked on dozens of folded paper napkins.*
*"First thing you have to do, Stevie, is clean up this*
*mess," I said. I tried not to sound stern.*

    *Stevie looked at me, and then at his mother, then*
*he pulled at one of the napkins. It had "Something For*
*Stevie" printed on it, and as he picked it up, two $10*
*bills fell onto the table. Stevie stared at the money, then*
*at all the napkins peeking from beneath the tableware,*
*each with his name printed or scrawled on it. I turned*
*to his mother. "There's more than $10,000 in cash and*
*checks on that table, all from truckers and trucking*
*companies that heard about your problems, so Happy*
*Thanksgiving!"*

    *Well, it got real noisy about that time, with every-*
*body hollering and shouting, and there were a few tears*
*as well. But you know what's funny? While everybody*
*else was busy shaking hands and hugging each other,*
*Stevie, with a big, big smile on his face, was busy clear-*
*ing all the cups and dishes from the table.*

    *Best worker I ever hired.*[6]

This story is not factual, and it can be found in many forms on the internet, but it speaks to us as Christians. Plant a seed and watch it grow.

    You know something — Job, in all his miseries, who was restored again to health and wealth; Cornelius the Roman officer; Simon Peter the great leader; and yes, the owner of a truck stop restaurant — today all cast their shadows of influence upon our lives and they with us rejoice when we discover new ways of accepting each other in the name of our Lord.

Yes! It is in the comfort of the shadow of an accepting God upon our lives that enables us to be more alive than ever.

As we look ahead Simon Peter is thrown into prison and his death seems imminent.

---

Please note that this study of Cornelius and Peter is divided into two parts. In its use as a Bible study in our home church it was well received and the class found it necessary because of time to look at it in two sections. The story easily lends itself to such a division and it is recommended that it be approached in such a manner.

1. Lloyd J. Ogilvie, *The Communicator's Commentary — Acts* (Waco: Word Books, 1983), p. 180. Through the years, I have known that a cubit was the distance from the tip of the fingers to the elbow, around eighteen inches. Fifty cubits would have been a distance of about 75 feet.

2. William Barclay, *The Acts of the Apostles* (Philadelphia: Westminster Press, 1955), pp. 83-84.

3. *Ibid*, p. 82.

4. Luke Timothy Johnson, *The Acts of the Apostles* (Collegeville, Minnesota: The Liturgical Press, 1992), p. 187.

5. The number of Jewish Christian believers is six according to Acts 11:12. One notes also that even though they were trying to find fault with Peter's approach to the Gentiles, Peter called them "brothers."

6. Dan Anderson, "Something For Stevie," published in *rpm for Truckers*, November 1998. It was reprised in Alice Gray's *Stories For A Faithful Heart* (Sisters, Oregon: Multnomah Publishers, 2000), pp. 22-25.

# Reflection And Discussion On Part 1

**Thought Questions**

1. How would you describe the faith of the Roman soldier, Cornelius?

2. How would you describe the attitude of the Jewish people to the Gentiles?

3. In what ways and through what channels does the Lord our God speak to us?

4. What are the requirements for people to be accepted into the Christian church membership today?

**Agree Or Disagree**

• Angels are only a part of the imagination of people today.

• Only Christians will be found in the kingdom of heaven.

• We should avoid having any contact with Muslims in America.

• Only English should be the official language of America.

• No one should be excommunicated from Christian church membership.

# Reflection And Discussion On Part 2

**Thought Questions**

1. What causes Simon Peter to really accept Cornelius and his family?

2. What do you think were the feelings of Cornelius and Peter when they met each other?

3. Why do you think Peter was invited to stay several more days with Cornelius and his family?

4. What practices in our church might be a barrier to some visitors feeling accepted?


**Agree Or Disagree**

• The sermon of Peter would be boring and uninteresting to people today.

• Even illegal immigrants should be accepted in our church.

• Speaking in tongues is an experience that deepens our faith.

• Speaking in tongues became a requirement for Gentiles to be a part of the church.

# Praying And Freedom Under The Shadow

*About that time King Herod laid violent hands upon some who belonged to the church. He had James, the brother of John, killed with the sword. After he saw that it pleased the Jews, he proceeded to arrest Peter also. (This was during the festival of Unleavened Bread.) When he had seized him, he put him in prison and handed him over to four squads of soldiers to guard him, intending to bring him out to the people after the Passover. While Peter was kept in prison, the church prayed fervently to God for him.* — Acts 12:1-5

*The very night before Herod was going to bring him out, Peter, bound with two chains, was sleeping between two soldiers, while guards in front of the door were keeping watch over the prison. Suddenly an angel of the Lord appeared and a light shone in the cell. He tapped Peter on the side and woke him, saying, "Get up quickly." And the chains fell off his wrists. The angel said to him, "Fasten your belt and put on your sandals." He did so. Then he said to him, "Wrap your cloak around you and follow me." Peter went out and followed him; he did not realize that what was happening with the angel's help was real; he thought he was seeing a vision. After they had passed the first and the second guard, they came before the iron gate leading into the city. It opened for them of its own accord, and they went outside and walked along a lane, when suddenly the angel left him. Then Peter came to himself and said, "Now I am sure that the Lord has sent his angel and rescued me from the hands of Herod and from all that the Jewish people were expecting."* — Acts 12:6-11

*As soon as he realized this, he went to the house of*
*Mary, the mother of John whose other name was Mark,*
*where many had gathered and were praying. When he*
*knocked at the outer gate, a maid named Rhoda came*
*to answer. On recognizing Peter's voice, she was so*
*overjoyed that, instead of opening the gate, she ran in*
*and announced that Peter was standing at the gate. They*
*said to her, "You are out of your mind!" But she in-*
*sisted that it was so. They said, "It is his angel." Mean-*
*while Peter continued knocking; and when they opened*
*the gate, they saw him and were amazed.*

*He motioned to them with his hand to be silent,*
*and described for them how the Lord had brought him*
*out of the prison. And he added, "Tell this to James*
*and to the believers." Then he left and went to another*
*place. When morning came, there was no small com-*
*motion among the soldiers over what had become of*
*Peter. When Herod had searched for him and could not*
*find him, he examined the guards and ordered them to*
*be put to death. Then he went down from Judea to*
*Caesarea and stayed there.*        — Acts 12:12-19

*For freedom Christ has set us free.*
*Stand firm, therefore, and do not submit again to a yoke of slavery.*
— Galatians 5:1

Believe it or not, there are such things as colored shadows. If white light is produced by separate colored light sources, the shadows are colored. Then we are told that in the absence of white light, colored lights blocked by an opaque surface, cast shadows in the colors complimentary to the lights blocked. For green light, red shadows and vice versa; for blue light, orange shadows and vice versa; for yellow light, purple shadows and vice versa. Wow! If you haven't seen this phenomenon it is hard to believe.

Peter's shadow is colored and dramatic in its influence on the development of the early church. We have seen how Peter's denial and then his experience of the risen Jesus on the shores of the Sea of Galilee assured him of his forgiveness and energized his spirit. After being filled with the power of the Holy Spirit on the day of Pentecost, he proclaimed such a powerful sermon that 3,000 people were baptized and the early church began. Peter continued his great leadership by healing the sick and proclaiming the good news of Jesus with great boldness even in the face of opposition and the threat of imprisonment. Under his ongoing leadership, the church became united and strong. Any threats of disloyalty and deceit were weeded out as in the case of Ananias and Sapphira. And yes, we have seen Peter through visions and much wrestling of mind and spirit become enabled to make the decision to accept the Roman centurion, Cornelius, and his family and friends into the fellowship and membership of the early church through their baptism and profession of faith.

The shadow of Simon Peter as it continued its influence upon the church was colored by great leadership, faithfulness, and conviction. Such qualities are further colored by Peter's ability to change his course of direction so that the bringing of the gospel of Jesus Christ begins to go out to all the people — both Jews and Gentiles.

**Persecution Under King Herod**

We return to our story and discover that the early Christian church now endures a time of persecution under King Herod Agrippa who was a grandson of Herod the Great and a nephew of Herod Antipas who had murdered John the Baptist. His opportunistic approach to leadership began during his training at Rome with the influence of Caligula, the selfish and egotistic son of the emperor. Finally he was appointed to rule in Palestine and was given power in stages, until he ruled over the largest realm of any man since his grandfather.[1] When you look at the history of Herod you discover he was a direct descendant of the Maccabees through his mother, Mariamne, and had learned to skillfully cultivate the favor of the Jewish people by meticulously keeping the law and all Jewish observances. In order to gain even further popularity with the Orthodox Jews, he begins a persecution of the Christians by having the apostle James beheaded.[2] For this act he received such praise from the leaders of the Jews he decided to go after the principal leader of the Christians, namely, Simon Peter. The city of Jerusalem was crowded with pilgrims from around the known world because of the Passover feast and what better time in the mind of Herod to imprison Peter and then to make a public spectacle of his execution.

### The Imprisonment Of Peter

Now we are face-to-face with a story that is not only full of drama and excitement, but also the unexpected. It is a story full of twists and turns as well as surprises and humor, and it is a story involving Christians gathered together in persistent prayer. In the dry and tough periods of life we, too, can pray expectantly, even impatiently, almost with a sense of resignation, only to discover that like those early Christians, we can be surprised at how God answers our prayers in remarkable ways, giving us a freedom and release we never envisioned.

As Herod carried out his plans to imprison Peter and then have him publicly executed, he wanted to make sure that there was no possible way that Peter could escape. So when Peter was imprisoned, he was placed in jail and bound not with one chain, but two. He was chained not to one soldier, but two. He had to sleep being chained between two soldiers! Furthermore, he was guarded by four squads of soldiers during the four watches of three hours each during the night. These soldiers would have been very zealous and careful in their guarding, because the law stated quite clearly that if a prisoner was allowed to escape, those who permitted it would suffer the same punishment as the prisoner. We are told that while Peter was kept in prison, the Christians gathered together and "prayed fervently to God for him" (Acts 12:5).

### The Praying Fellowship

Surely those who prayed felt that it would almost be impossible for Peter to escape. In a sense, there was nothing those people could do but pray. Their own lives were in danger, also! I am sure they prayed that somehow Peter could be released and not killed, and yet the prayers would have been with a sense of resignation, almost despair. After all, the great apostle James had already been beheaded, and they had prayed for him. Even so, they could at least pray that Peter be sustained and strengthened in this ordeal. At the same time, I am sure that the Christians who gathered to pray were quite aware of many answered prayers and that given the circumstances they and Peter were facing — there was no more powerful weapon than prayer.

One of the problems that we all face is not how to pray, but what we should pray in the face of suffering, sickness, and great ordeals including dying and death. In my calling on the sick and the dying through the years, whenever the doctors let it be known that a person's illness was final and that death was near, it never seemed appropriate to pray for a miraculous cure. Rather, there was a committal of the person into the hands of a merciful and loving God and the conviction that nothing, not even death, could separate us from the love and presence of our God.

Lloyd Ogilvie who served many years as senior pastor of the First Presbyterian Church in Hollywood, California, and then went on to become the Chaplain of the United States Senate, knows something about praying daily for others and especially the leaders of our country. It is helpful to me when he comments on the Christians praying for Peter with these words:

> *When a person we love is troubled, we wonder what is best. We are reluctant to be specific in our intercession because we fear telling God what we think is best. We get into the muddle of what's our will versus what is God's will, as if the two could not be the same. Years of trying to learn how and what to pray for others have taught me to spend more time listening to what the Lord wants me to ask than in asking. Then the asking can be what He is more ready to give than I may have the courage to ask.*[3]

How well I remember a woman in one of my parishes who was in her eighties and yet in the best of condition, in fact, she even went jogging several times a week. One day she developed a severe infection in one of her legs and it became worse and worse until finally there was no solution but to amputate the leg. After the leg had been amputated, and great healing had taken place, she was fitted with a prosthetic and was finally able to be quite active. After another period of time, her other leg became infected and had to be amputated as well. When I visited her after the surgery I asked her how she felt and if she had any severe pain, she replied, "You know ... what little is left of me is pretty good!" As a pastor praying for healing it was uplifting to see her radiant faith and spirit even though her legs were not spared. I believe that when it comes to praying for others we need to listen carefully and then to ask boldly, knowing that whatever the answer, it is part of God's plan and purpose.

**An Escape From Prison**

As we return to Peter's imprisonment, we come face-to-face with an exciting account of an escape into freedom. An angel appears in Peter's cell and a light surrounds them. We can't help noticing that Peter is sound asleep, in fact, so deep in sleep that he has to be jarred awake! Even though he is between two soldiers and knows that his execution is near, he sleeps with a great trust in our God. The angel treats him as if caring for a child telling him to get up quickly, at which time the chains fell off his wrists. Then he is told to fasten his belt and to put on his sandals and then to wrap his cloak around him in order to be prepared for the cold night air. They simply walked by the first and second stations of guards and then outside. When they approached the gate into the city, it opened of its own accord. Not until Peter found himself walking down a street in Jerusalem did he come fully to his senses and realized an angel of the Lord had helped him and he had been set free! Peter, with the miraculous help of God, had gone from the chains of imprisonment to freedom and from certain death to life, and it produced within him an exuberant kind of joy and thanksgiving.

Peter now sought out his brothers and sisters in Christ for he wanted to share with them his newfound joy and freedom. That's the way Peter was! Since the day of Pentecost when he had been filled with the power of the Spirit, he was always eager to share with others not only his joys but his failures and mistakes, as well.

When the realization came to him that he really was free, he made his way to the home of the mother of John Mark, the site of the upper room, and the place where the Christians were gathered together in prayer for Peter.

What follows is filled with joy and humor. There was an outer court that surrounded the home with a great fence and a heavy wooden gate that was the only way to get into the home and of course, it was tightly locked. Every precaution for safety had been taken to make certain that those gathered within would be protected from Herod and his soldiers. In the middle of the night we find Peter knocking and knocking at the gate and looking around the empty street expecting the soldiers to come after him at any moment.

We are told that a young woman by the name of Rhoda was sent by the Christians gathered to see who could possibly be at the gate. She is startled to hear the voice of Peter from the other side of the gate and she becomes so excited that instead of unlocking the gate she runs back to tell them that Peter is there! Although they have been praying for Peter, they look at Rhoda incredulously. They believe that in the danger of the moment, she has completely lost her senses and so they say to her, "You are out of your mind!" Really, the original Greek word here has them saying, "You are out of touch with reality." But when she insists that Peter is really there they reply that it must be his angel. It was believed in those days that everyone had a guardian angel and so the people either believed that the angel was doing his job of protecting and strengthening Peter, or worse yet, that Peter had already been beheaded and that it was his spirit at the gate.

Peter kept knocking persistently and I'm sure continued to look anxiously around. When they finally let Peter inside they were astonished beyond measure and were filled with praise and thanksgiving and unbelievable joy as they listened to their beloved Peter tell of his miraculous escape from imprisonment and certain death.

Before Peter left to find a safe hiding place for a time he gave the group an interesting command, "Tell this to James and to the believers." This James was the brother of Jesus who had become the president of the church. We remind ourselves that Jesus had four brothers whose names were: James, Joses, Judas, and Simon, along with at least two sisters. During the public ministry of Jesus, these brothers did not support him and they actually thought that he was mad and often took offense at him (Mark 6:3; John 7:5). But something happened when Jesus was killed. Perhaps James as the next oldest brother watched Jesus die and was strongly influenced by how he died and what happened afterward. The apostle Paul speaks of the resurrection appearances of Jesus saying that first of all he appeared to Peter, then to the twelve, and then to more than 500 brothers and sisters at one time, most of them still alive — indicating that they could have been 500 youth. Then Paul said Jesus appeared to his brother James, and then to all the apostles (1 Corinthians 15:3-7). It strikes me that this appearance of the resurrected Jesus to his brother must have been very emotional and meaningful and certainly affected James the rest of his life. I am sure that Jesus, after his death, singling out his brother, James, freed him from the chains of misunderstanding and gave him a whole new abundant life. Peter, now freed from his prison, wants this James to know of his escape from prison and death and that it happened miraculously by the power of God. And such a power is available to you and to me.

**The Power To Escape From That Which Imprisons Us**

My friends, from the time that we are young we can be chained down by our fears, even small ones. I want to affirm that God's help can come to us even through the very young. Come with me to a third-grade classroom. There is an eight-year-old boy sitting at his desk and all of a sudden there is a puddle between his feet and the front of his pants are wet. He thinks his heart is going to stop because he cannot possibly imagine how this has happened. It has never happened before, and he knows that when the boys find out he will never hear the end of it. When the girls find out, they'll never speak to him again as long as he lives.

The boy believes his heart is going to stop; he puts his head down and prays this prayer, "Dear God, this is an emergency! I need help now! Five minutes from now I'm dead meat."

He looks up from his prayer and here comes the teacher with a look in her eyes that says he has been discovered. As the teacher is walking toward him, a classmate named Susie is carrying a goldfish bowl that is filled with water. Susie trips in front of the teacher and inexplicably dumps the bowl of water in the boy's lap. The boy pretends to be angry, but all the while is saying to himself, "Thank you, Lord! Thank you, Lord!"

Now, instead of being the object of ridicule, the boy is the object of sympathy. The teacher rushes him downstairs and gives him gym shorts to put on while his pants dry out. All the other children are on their hands and knees cleaning up around his desk. The sympathy is wonderful. But as life would have it, the ridicule that should have been his has been transferred to someone else — Susie. She tries to help, but they tell her to get out. "You've done enough, you klutz!"

Finally, at the end of the day, as they are waiting for the bus, the boy walks over to Susie and whispers, "You did that on purpose, didn't you?" Susie whispers back, "I wet my pants once, too."

I believe from the time we are very young, we can be imprisoned by fears that can be relieved by the Lord our God working through someone else. You and I can be instruments of the Lord God freeing someone else from their fears and in the process we all become more alive than ever.

No matter how old we are, there are many things that can enslave and imprison us. There are many things that can keep us from the abundant overflowing life that Jesus wants for you and me. We can be enslaved by drugs and addictions of all kinds. Every twelve-step program that I have seen reminds us that we can't overcome the enslavement by ourselves. We need a higher power and for many of you dear readers — it is to have a new and restored relationship with Jesus as Lord and Savior. We can be enslaved by fears of all kinds and by physical, mental, and emotional handicaps. The Lord our God can help us as he helped Peter of old to break our chains and scale the heights of endurance we have never known before.

From the time he was 25 years old, Tom Whitaker, who resides in Scottsdale, Arizona, has focused his life on being a climber. At first he experimented with climbing higher and higher rocks, then the steep hills, and finally the mountains. But his career as a climber of high places appeared to hit rock bottom when he was involved in a collision with a drunken driver on Thanksgiving Day in 1974. After the crash, he was hospitalized with two shattered legs and a severed foot and wound up with severely damaged knees, which caused him to have his right kneecap removed and his right foot amputated.

"I was a bag of broken bones in a hospital, and people would sit beside me and weep," said Whitaker. "They had written me off. They figured I'd never climb again." However, inside of Tom Whitaker was God's great gift of endurance and with the aid of a special prosthetic device he learned to walk and climb higher and higher each day. Within his goal of two years, he climbed the Outer Limits in Yosemite (Valley, California) and then set his sights on the ultimate challenge for a mountain climber: Mount Everest. His first two attempts to reach the top of the world's tallest peak were unsuccessful. But on May 27, 1998, he completed the ascent, becoming the first disabled person in history to reach the top, where he deposited a rock that had been given to him by a teammate who said to him, "I want you to take this rock to the very top of the mountain where it belongs!"

On November 4, 2006, he received an award from Queen Elizabeth II of his native England during an investiture ceremony at Buckingham Palace. She honored Whitaker for his service to disabled people and for inspiring them to break some of the chains of their restrictions and also for his ongoing service to mountain climbers. He recalls the special decorations of the palace and most vividly he remembers almost tripping before the queen!

"I knew the protocol about not putting your back to her, so I had to walk backward when we were done," he said. "I was worried that with the prosthesis I might trip. Here I am getting an award for mountain climbing and I had visions of falling flat on my face in front of the Queen."[4] Yes, fears and disabilities could have imprisoned him for life, but God's great gifts of endurance and desire gave him and can give us a whole new life of freedom. Simon Peter knew all about imprisonments and the threats of death. His miraculous escape from prison gave him a new sense of freedom within. Certainly he had the freedom to act on his convictions for he knew the risen Lord was with him, no matter what, and now nothing could prevent him from preaching the gospel not only to the Jews, but also to the Gentiles and to the world. Under the mighty colored and colorful shadow of Simon Peter we can be freed up to go and tell the story of God's love and mercy to our children and our children's children.

Believe it or not there are such things as colored shadows.

———————

1. Lloyd J. Ogilvie, *The Communicator's Commentary — Acts* (Waco: Word Books, 1983), p. 197.

2. William Barclay, *The Acts of the Apostles* (Philadelphia: Westminster Press, 1955), pp. 98-102.

3. *Op cit*, Ogilvie, pp. 198-199.

4. This story is from the *East Valley Tribune*, Mesa, Arizona, December 11, 2006.

# Reflection And Discussion

## Thought Questions

1. What was the reaction of the early church to Peter's imprisonment?

2. What are the things that imprison us and keep us from the abundant life?

3. How do we break away from those things that imprison us?

4. How do you feel about the fact that God saved Peter and not the apostle James?

## Agree Or Disagree

• We should always end a prayer for healing with the words, "If it be your will."

• Oftentimes we pray for something not really expecting an answer.

• God always hears and answers prayer.

• The more persistent we are in prayer the more answers we receive.

• Group prayer is more powerful than praying alone.

# Postscript

The story of Simon Peter comes to a climax in his appearance before a great assembly of the apostles and elders of the early church in the city of Jerusalem. There was a burning issue that consumed their thinking and that called for some kind of a major decision. It concerned the Gentiles and how they should be received into the fellowship and membership of the church. The orthodox Jewish leaders believed that these Gentiles should first be immersed into the teachings, rules, regulations, and rituals of Judaism and then that the men should be circumcised. Peter and the apostles and many others felt that belief in the risen Jesus as Lord and Savior, followed by baptism, was all that was necessary. After much heated debate at this assembly, Peter stood and said to those gathered:

> *My brothers, you know that in the early days God made a choice among you, that I should be the one through whom the Gentiles would hear the message of the good news and become believers. And God, who knows the human heart, testified to them by giving them the Holy Spirit, just as he did to us; and in cleansing their hearts by faith he has made no distinction between them and us. Now therefore why are you putting God to the test by placing on the neck of the disciples a yoke that neither our ancestors nor we have been able to bear? On the contrary, we believe that we will be saved through the grace of the Lord Jesus, just as they will.*
>
> — Acts 15:7-11

Peter's words and fervor greatly influenced the assembly and the result has affected and infected the church to the present moment. The gospel of Jesus Christ was not to be confined in the arms of Judaism, but was meant to be proclaimed to all people. As an old song proclaimed, "Red or yellow, black or white, they are precious in his sight." Christianity was free to be proclaimed to all people and to the whole world as well as worlds to come!

One of the aspects of Peter's life that brought him to the conclusion that the gospel of Jesus Christ must be proclaimed to all people was the struggles and sufferings of his life that molded and shaped his convictions. My good friend, Paul Werger, who was my fellow pastor in Minnesota for many years and who became our bishop in Iowa and is now retired as bishop emeritus, has spoken often of the sufferings that shaped Peter's life and lengthened his shadow of healing and compassion upon all who listen to his words. All of us face struggles and sufferings of all kinds and the shadow of Peter upon us can be very helpful in enabling us to become more alive than ever.

In our conversations together, Paul Werger spoke about and has written of the following areas of Peter's suffering.

- The price he paid in dropping everything to follow Jesus — including a good fishing trade.
- The sufferings of his wife when her husband left her to go gallivanting around with that new prophet from Nazareth.
- The humiliation when Jesus rebuked him with "Get behind me, Satan! You are a stumbling block to me; for you are setting your mind not on divine things but on human things." Words that stopped Peter in his tracks after he had been thrilled by the words of Jesus to him after he had recognized Jesus as the Messiah when he said, "Blessed are you Simon son of Jonah! For flesh and blood has not revealed this to you, but my Father in heaven. And I tell you, you are Peter, and on this rock I will build my church, and the gates of Hades will not prevail against it" (Acts 16:23; 16:16-18). Yes, to be affirmed and then to be put down is a deep kind of hurt.
- The agony and regret of discovering that he was a real coward when he denied Jesus three times and then heard the cock crow.[1]

Yes, suffering was a part of Peter's life all the way to the end and this knowledge adds a new kind of comfort for us in what he says and does. Following Peter's stirring witness to the Jerusalem assembly of the early church, he disappears from the book of Acts and we are not told what happened further in his life. Yet there remain unanimous traditions about his ongoing life and ministry. For example, he is strongly associated with the followers of Jesus in the city of Antioch where, you will remember, the believers in Jesus were first called "Christians." We are told that Peter was the first bishop of the church in Antioch and served there for seven years.

Peter is also connected with the church in Asia Minor. The first letter of Peter in the scriptures is said to have been written by Peter or someone who wanted to honor his name and who was closely related to his preaching and teaching. It is addressed to Christians scattered throughout Pontus, Galatia, Cappadocia, Asia, and Bithynia. In this letter there is mention of the city of Babylon, which is a code word for Rome and was used to make it known that the size and wickedness of Rome was comparable to ancient Babylon.

The greatest and most repeated tradition of the early church that comes down to us today is that Peter for certain, after preaching the gospel throughout Asia Minor, and even in the city of Corinth came to the city of Rome. According to many scholars this was about 61 AD, and while in Rome, Peter preached to both Jews and Gentiles.[2] During his time in the great city there came a terrible wave of persecution because of the Emperor Nero. Peter was urged by his friends and followers to flee the city so that his life could be spared and so that he could return to serve again. What happened next is an extremely strong and unanimous legend that has come down through the centuries and continues to stir the hearts of Christians today. When Peter fled the city along the Appian Way, he noticed a man coming back into the city, and when he came close Peter recognized him as the risen Christ and so he exclaimed,

*"Where are you going, Lord?"*
*"I am going into Rome to be crucified!"*
*"Lord, are you going to be crucified again?"*
*"Yes, Peter, I am being crucified again."*

111

Peter understood the words of Jesus to mean that since he was fleeing his time of martyrdom, Jesus, his beloved Lord, was now going to take his place. Peter went back into the city and, yes, he was captured along with his wife. When the time for the crucifixion came, Peter was forced to look upon the crucifixion of his wife first. Over and over again he tried to comfort her saying, "Remember the Lord. Remember the Lord!"[3]

Now when it was time for Peter to be crucified he asked to be crucified with his head downward because he felt he was not worthy to die as the Lord had died. In fact, Peter conducted himself with such courage that even his jailer was moved to accept the Christian faith.

Two traditional burial places exist for Peter. One is under the Cathedral of Saint Peter on Vatican Hill. The other is thought to be in the catacombs of the Basilica of Saint Sebastian on the Appian Way.

One of the great preachers in the early church was a man called Chrysostom (347-407) and I agree with him when he writes, "Peter is the mouthpiece of the disciples, the leader of the apostolic chorus — the pillar of the church, the basis of faith, the foundation of our confession, the worldwide fisherman who brought our race heavenward from the abyss of error."[4]

Simon Peter, indeed, is a fisher of people everywhere. He proclaimed the gospel of Jesus our Lord and Savior in Jerusalem, Samaria, Lydda, Joppa, Caesarea, Pontus, Galatia, Cappadocia, Asia, Bithynia, Antioch, Corinth, Rome, and to our world and the worlds to come.

Stirring words in the letters of Peter in the Bible surely were heard from his lips and continue to be heard today. When I am discouraged or anxious, I hear Peter say, "Humble yourselves therefore under the mighty hand of God, so that he may exalt you in due time. Cast all your anxiety on him, because he cares for you" (1 Peter 5:6-7). And when I feel alone and weak, I hear Peter saying, "You are a chosen race, a royal priesthood, a holy nation, God's own people, in order that you may proclaim the mighty acts of him who called you out of darkness into his marvelous light — now you are God's people — now you have received mercy" (1 Peter 2:9-10).

Alleluia! Amen.

---

1. These words came out of conversations with my good friend Dr. Paul Werger who is retired as Bishop Emeritus of the Southeastern Iowa Synod of the Evangelical Lutheran Church in America.

2. John H. Baumgaertner, *Meet the Twelve* (Minneapolis: Augsburg Publishing House, 1960), pp. 121-122.

3. William Barclay, *The Master's Men* (New York-Nashville: Abingdon Press, 1959), pp. 26-27.

4. Asbury Smith, *The Twelve Christ Chose* (New York: Harper & Brothers, 1958), pp. 21-22.

# Epilogue
# Simon Peter's Monologue

### Prologue To Simon Peter

We invite into our midst one of the greatest of the disciples whom the world knows as Simon Peter. This disciple, more than any other, can teach us many things. His impulsive words and actions, his eager exclamations and confessions, his sometimes manly and cowardly acts, his oaths, his bitter tears ... all this makes Peter the great companion and instructor of us all.

Listen to him again as he shares with us the close intimate moments he had with our Lord. May you feel the wind and the waves of the Sea of Galilee, hear the crowds and commotion of Capernaum, and see the dazzling light of the Mountain of Transfiguration. Follow this disciple into the anguish and fear of Gethsemane and to the suffering of the cross.

Enter with him into the valley of despair as he falls before a simple question. Know again that every moment we face brings with it the possibility of our own denial of Jesus in thought, word, or deed. Then experience with Peter the power of the risen Lord who restores and renews and empowers and forgives.

We welcome this disciple into our midst and listen to his story.

### Simon Peter — "I Denied Him"

My name is Simon Bar Jonah, a name that means son of Jonah, or John, as you would say. Our father was a fisherman by trade and his business became prosperous and widespread all the way to Jerusalem. My brother, Andrew, and I grew up along the shores of the Sea of Galilee and so we became strong and rugged from the wind and waves and the pull of the nets.

How I would like to take you to such a place of beauty. That lake was located several hundred feet (686) below sea level and helped produce a warm and balmy climate tempered by the cool breezes off the water. This body of water was harp shaped and in your measurements was thirteen miles long and eight miles wide at its widest point. There were 32 miles of shoreline with rugged hills, woods, gardens, and nine key cities. Such a place bustled with activity. The waters were clear, sparkling blue, and deep, nearly 170 feet. How we loved to fish for the carp and catfish, the comb fish, sardine, and mullet.

One day I was seated beside the shore mending the breaks in the fishnets with new flaxen cord. My brother, Andrew, came running up with breathless excitement and said, "Simon, we have found the one of whom Moses and the prophets spoke. We have found the Messiah!"

"Come now," I said to my brother, "The Messiah is not likely to be found in these parts or at this time of history."

My brother knew better than to argue with me and just said, "Simon, come and see."

We walked down the shore a ways and came to a sheltered cove. There stood this Jesus and he turned to me and acted as if he had always known me. "So, you are Simon, son of John. You will be called Peter the Rock."

We followed him for a while and we heard wondrous words and stories and saw great miracles of healing. Yet we had a fishing business and had to return to the lake. Some time went by and one day we saw Jesus walking along the shore. We didn't even know that he had returned. He called out to us, "Follow me, and I will make you become fishers of others." By the grace of God my life turned in the right direction and I left everything behind. My friends, I have so many memories — but time permits me to share just a few.

One day, Jesus was teaching a great crowd in the city of Capernaum located on the northern shores of the Sea of Galilee. Suddenly, there came the leader of the synagogue, a man by the name of Jairus, shoving and pushing his way through the crowd. "Jesus," he said, "come quickly, my daughter is close to death." I never saw Jesus turn down anyone and so we went with Jairus through the city streets. As we approached his home, we heard the flute players and the sounds of the mourners and we knew the daughter was dead. I remember that Jesus turned to Jairus and said, "Do not be afraid, but believe!" Jesus took James and John along with myself and we went into the home with the parents to an upper chamber where lay this twelve-year-old girl who had died. I remember that Jesus took her by the hand and said in Aramaic, "*Talitha, cumi*," which means, "Little girl, I say to you arise." And she stood up and lived!

You know there were days in which I thought I knew who this Jesus really was. Desiring to teach us as disciples, he took us one day to the region of Caesarea Philippi, north and east of the Sea of Galilee. There, away from the crowds, he asked us, "Who do the people say that I am?" We quickly answered, "Jesus, they think that you are Jeremiah, or Elijah, or one of the prophets. Some even think that you are John the Baptist come back alive again." Then he pointed at us and asked, "But who do *you* say that I am?" It grew quiet and I couldn't help myself. I spoke up and said, "You are the Messiah, the Son of the living God." Jesus turned to me and said, "Blessed are you, Simon Bar Jonah, for flesh and blood has not revealed this to you, but my Father who is in heaven. On you and your rock like faith I will build my church and the gates of death will not prevail against her."

Then there were days in which I was full of questions and doubts and wondered. Jesus kept saying that he had to go to Jerusalem and that there the chief priests and scribes would turn against him and that he would be killed. I said to him, "God forbid that this should ever happen to you." And he turned on me and said, "Get behind me, Satan. You are a stumbling block to me for you are not on the side of God but on the side of others." I was crushed, but you see I did not want him to die. I loved him. Jesus went on to teach us that those who believe in him must take up a cross and follow him and that those who try to save their lives will lose them, and that those who lose their lives for him will find them.

As time went on, Jesus seemed to become increasingly troubled. One day he said to me, "Go, get James and John and come and follow me." We journeyed northward from the Sea of Galilee some fifty miles to the majestic slopes of Mount Hermon that rises some 11,000 feet above the Jordan Valley. On a clear day, you can see it 100 miles away at the Dead Sea. It took us several days and when we arrived, we climbed to a plateau far above the valley. Jesus went further ahead of us and began to pray. As he did so, he suddenly changed. His dusty garments became white as snow and his face began to shine like the sun. There appeared speaking to him none other than Moses and Elijah. Later we would find out that they were speaking about the valley and the cross. I shouted out, "Jesus it is good for you to be here, let me make three shelters — one for you, one for Moses, and one for Elijah."

Suddenly a cloud enveloped us and we heard the voice of God the Father like the sound of many waters, "This is my beloved Son, listen to him!" We were so frightened that we fell to the ground and hid our faces. It grew quiet and all I could hear was the sound of the wind through the grass. Feeling a touch on my shoulder, I looked up and saw no one except Jesus with the same dusty garments and ready now for the valley below. My friends, I hope that you, too, would hear again the voice of God the Father saying: "This is my beloved Son, listen to him!" And, of course, you can listen to him through the scriptures, and when you pray, and when you come here to this place of worship. And you can listen to him when you reach out to someone close to you. Yes, today, you can find Jesus and listen to him among those in need.

I must hasten on now to the night of my terrible failure. Jesus most earnestly desired to celebrate with us the Passover feast. Careful arrangements were made in the upper room in Jerusalem. Late in the afternoon we were walking toward this home when we as disciples began to argue with each other as to who was going to be the greatest in the kingdom that Jesus would establish. By the time we arrived at the upper room, we were sullen, silent, and angry with each other. Jesus met us at the door and took a towel and a basin of water and kneeling before each of us he washed our dirty, dusty feet.

As he knelt before me, I said, "Jesus, you shouldn't wash my feet."

"Simon, if I don't wash your feet you can have no part of me."

"Then, Jesus, wash my hands and my head!"

Through this washing, Jesus was teaching us that whoever would be the greatest must be the servant of all.

As we celebrated the Passover meal together, Jesus seemed to become increasingly troubled. Then he said, "One of you will betray me." We all said, "Is it I? Is it I?" I remember that Jesus took some bread, dipped it, and gave it to Judas. He seemed to get up and leave rather suddenly — but we didn't think much about it. After all, he was our treasurer and there were always money matters and bills to be paid.

Then Jesus took some bread, broke it, and gave thanks. He gave it to us and said, "Take and eat, this is my body given for you. Do this often to remember me." Then he took the chalice of wine and passed it to us saying, "This cup is the new covenant in my blood given and shed for you. Drink of it, all of you, to remember me, and to receive forgiveness."

Jesus began to teach us many things about the kingdom. Suddenly he singled me out, "Simon, Satan desires to have you and to sift you like wheat. I am praying for you that when you are strengthened you will be able to strengthen the others." Inwardly, I didn't understand what he was saying and wondered why he was picking on me. As the night grew late, there was an increasing fear and uneasiness in our hearts. We just knew that he was going to be killed. Jesus said, "Let not your hearts be troubled. In my Father's house are many dwelling places. I go to prepare a place for you that where I am you may be also." After singing a hymn, we went out into the city streets. There was a sense of death and foreboding in the air. A full moon tried to shimmer through the dark clouds.

As we walked along, Jesus sighed and said, "All of you will run away because of me."

"Jesus, even if they all run away, I will not."

"Simon, before the cock crow sounds twice, you will deny me three times."

"Jesus, even if I must die with you, I will not deny you."

It was not a lightly given promise. But things began to happen quickly. We climbed down into the Kidron Valley. Crossing the brook we climbed up the Mount of Olives about a third of the way to the garden called Gethsemane. Jesus left the other disciples outside and took James and John and myself further into the garden. We could tell that Jesus wasn't himself. He began to tremble like a leaf and the perspiration of his brow was like drops of blood. We heard him say, "My soul is sorrowful unto death." He went about a stone's throw away and flung himself upon the ground and we heard him cry out, "Father, remove this cup." But our eyes grew heavy in the darkness and I fell soundly asleep. Jesus came back and awakened me saying, "Simon, can you not watch with me one hour." Three times this happened. Suddenly, I awakened and I saw them coming. There were the torches and the priests and servants, and soldiers with their clubs and swords. And there was Judas! He came forward and kissed Jesus! I took my sword and swung wildly trying to defend him. I cut off the ear of Malchus, the servant of the high priest, but Jesus made me put my sword away and took the man's ear and healed it. Then he said to me, "Simon, do you not know that I can defend myself? I can call upon twelve legions of angels." Yes, they took him! And yes, we all fled!

John and I came to our senses and followed him from a distance. We saw them take Jesus into the home of the high priest. John was well known there from fishing days and went inside and convinced a maid at the door to let me in. You know, if someone had said to me in that moment, "Simon, watch out, there are enemies inside." I would have said, "I can take care of myself!" I went to the outer courtyard. It was cold that night and someone had made a charcoal fire, so I went over and warmed my hands. As I look back, I suspect my face was outlined by the flames. A maid said, "Surely you are one of those followers of Jesus." Now if I thought anything at all, I thought I needed to be careful lest I got John into trouble. Some time later, one of the bystanders said, "You must be one of the disciples of Jesus." I took an oath and said, "I don't know the man." Then a servant of the high priest said, "You are one of those followers of Jesus. Your Galilean accent gives you away." It was then that I cursed and swore and said, "I don't know the man!" It grew very quiet to me and all I could hear was the distant cock crow. Never did it seem so loud.

A door opened and Jesus was led by and he turned and looked at me. Oh, I wish I could tell you all about that look. There was pain but no indignation. There was disappointment, but there was forgiveness and love. That look was like a mirror in which I saw myself as I really was — a coward and a traitor. However, it was also a window through which I saw the loving heart of Jesus. Strong man that I was, I went out and wept bitterly. Ah, the world knows of my failure and denial. But it also knows of my remorse and repentance.

The next day was Friday. By 9 o'clock in the morning, they had crucified this bloodied Jesus between two thieves on a hill outside the city. At noon, dark clouds rolled in and darkness covered the site and a terrible storm arose. By 3:00 in the afternoon, Jesus breathed his last. Still the soldiers came and rammed a spear in his side and blood and water poured out. I remember that Joseph of Arimathea and Nicodemus came with permission to take down the body. They buried Jesus in Joseph's garden in a cave and placed a stone before the entrance and sealed it — and all of our dreams and hopes were broken and finished!

My friends, early Sunday morning, there came a pounding at the door. It was the women saying that they had visited the tomb and the stone was rolled away and the body was gone! John and I raced to the tomb. John was younger and got there first and stood looking inside. When I arrived I brushed past John and went into the tomb. When my eyes became accustomed to the gloom, I saw an astounding sight. The grave cloths that had surrounded the body of Jesus still lay in their folds. The cloth that had been around his head, had been taken off. It was carefully folded and laid to the side. We saw! We wondered!

Days went by and I was feeling restless. I said to the others, "I don't know about you, but I'm going fishing." Nathaniel and Thomas, James and John, and a couple of the others joined me. We journeyed northward to the Sea of Galilee. How good it was to be out upon the sea and to feel the wind and the waves and the nets. Ah, but we fished all through the night and caught nothing. In the early hours of the morning as the dawn broke and the mist arose we were only a hundred yards from the shore. We saw the figure of a man standing there and he called out to us.

"Have you caught any fish?"

"No!"

"Then let down your nets on the other side."

121

As we did so, we enclosed such a school of fish that the nets were almost breaking. John looked at him and said to me, "It is the Lord!" I leaped into the water and waded ashore. There stood this risen and alive Jesus. He had made a charcoal fire and a breakfast for us of fish and bread. Afterward Jesus singled me out.

"Simon, do you love me more than these things?"

"Yes, Lord, you know that I love you."

"Then, Simon, feed my lambs."

Three times he asked me that question, "Simon, do you love me more than these things?" And three times I answered, "Yes, Lord, you know that I love you." And Jesus answered, "Feed my lambs! Tend my sheep! Feed my sheep!" In that moment I, Simon, knew that Jesus was reminding me of my threefold denial. But I also knew that he was forgiving, restoring, and renewing me. I, Simon, who had such feet of clay, became Peter with a rocklike faith.

I must go now, and I hope my life says some things to you. First of all, watch out for those old sinful habits. I had not cursed or swore for a long time, but it all came back to me in a moment of weakness. Jesus can help you not only to bury old sinful habits but set a guard before them. Then take the time to pray. Jesus wanted me to watch and pray, and I only slept. And may my life remind you to be careful about the company you keep.

I found myself surrounded by the enemies of Jesus, and by those who didn't know him and made fun of him. I tried to be like them. My friends do not deny Jesus in this way. Most of all, never give in to despair. Jesus is alive. Jesus is here. Again he says, "Come to me, all you who are heavy laden and weighed down with guilt and worry. Come to me, and I will give you rest." In fact, Jesus says that he will be there beyond your next sin and failure. "Don't despair," he says, "I want to forgive, restore, renew, and empower you." That's the kind of Savior he was to me. That's the kind of Savior he wants to be to you.

I, Simon Peter, bid you farewell. The Lord be with you.

## Suggestions For Presentation

1.  It is important to memorize the script thoroughly and then to find a place to say it out loud over and over again. Initially, it could easily take ten times before the words become a part of you. When they do, you will feel like Peter. You will act like Peter. You will, in a sense, become Peter. I made this presentation annually for almost thirty years in other congregations and in my own congregation on Maundy Thursday in the season of Lent. Each year it was easier to memorize and soon it became such a part of me that it was easy to make new changes and adaptations.

2.  The Prologue is meant to be an introduction that helps to prepare the listeners for what is to happen. It needs to be read by someone other than yourself. Make sure it is a person who is an excellent reader.

3.  To become Simon Peter requires a good costume. All of our key cities have costume houses that will require your measurements and will rent you a costume that will fit perfectly. The first time you should take it on and off two or three times so you can find out the best and most efficient way to do so. At the time of the presentation you don't need the frustration of trying to figure out the correct way of putting it on. Believe me — I know how that can happen! Hopefully you have a portable microphone system that has a power box you can clip to your belt. The pocket slits in the sides of the robe enable you to clip the small microphone within the folds of the robe. After presenting Simon Peter for several years, I was fortunate to have the president of the altar guild, who was a great seamstress, make me a robe. Another family presented me with a pair of leather strapped sandals that added to the authenticity of the presentation. I hope the same thing happens to you!

4.  Make good use of light and darkness. Usually in the Lenten season it gets dark early, which is a great help to the presentation. Toward the end of the prologue, the lights were slowly

brought down. When there is almost darkness, the character of Peter can step out into the center. Once in place a spotlight in the balcony or in the back can be turned on. This shift from light to darkness to spotlight as in a theater transports the congregation and sets the mood for the presentation. If you do not have a spotlight, the purchase of one will be a great help for other presentations like concerts, plays, Christmas programs, and so on.

5. Make use of music off a disc that can be played through your sound system. I found a marvelous pastoral music piece from Mozart that did much to set the mood. It started toward the end of the prologue softly and then made a crescendo as the lights were dimmed to darkness. The music was used also at the end of the monologue.

6. Makeup is important. You should use enough to give you a tanned appearance. Make sure that you also put it on your feet. Your feet will be barefoot in the leather strapped sandals and white feet, I have discovered, are noticed and are a distraction. I also learned early on that white feet subtract from the authenticity of the presentation! If you are young you might also want to use a makeup pencil to insert some wrinkles! Starting with the Lenten season I always grew a beard that was always quite full by the time of Holy Week. My beard was very dark so I used white shoe polish to add the needed gray. By the way, the white shoe polish comes out easily in the shower!

7. I know that all this sounds like a lot of work, and it certainly is. You will need a small group of people to help you with the details. When you have finished the monologue of Simon Peter, you will know that you have been Peter and that the audience has had a moving and soaring experience of renewed faith. Furthermore, the crowds of people will grow each year. People love being moved and lifted. So will you!

124

# Bibliography

Awwad, Sami. *The Holy Land in Colour*. Jerusalem: Palphot, Ltd., 1975.

Barclay, William. *The Gospel of Matthew*, vol. 2. Philadelphia: Westminster Press, 1957, 1958.

Barclay, William. *The Gospel of Mark*. Philadelphia: Westminster Press, 1954, 1956.

Barclay, William. *The Gospel of Luke*. Philadelphia: Westminster Press, 1953, 1956.

Barclay, William. *The Gospel of John,* vol. 2. Louisville: Westminster John Knox Press, 1975.

Barclay, William. *The Acts of the Apostles*. Philadelphia, Westminster Press, 1955.

Barclay, William. *The Letters of James and Peter*. Philadelphia: Westminster Press, 1976.

Barclay, William. *The Master's Men's*. Nashville: Abingdon Press, 1959.

Baumgaertner, John H. *Meet the Twelve*. Minneapolis: Augsburg Publishing House. 1960.

Bowker, John. *The Complete Bible Handbook*. London, New York: PK Publishing, Inc., 1998.

Buttrick, George Arthur. *The Interpreter's Dictionary of the Bible*, vol. 1, 4. Nashville: Abingdon Press, 1962.

Buttrick, George Arthur. *The Interpreter's Bible*. Nashville: Abingdon Press, 1951, 1952.

Derrett, J. M. D. "Ananias, Sapphira, and the Right of Property," *Downside Review 89*, 1971.

Dossey, Larry, M.D. *Healing Words*. San Francisco: HarperCollins, 1993.

Dupont, J. *Community of Goods in the Early Church*. New York: Paulist Press, 1979.

Heim, Ralph D. *A Harmony of the Gospels*. Philadelphia: Fortress Press, 1947.

Hobart, William K. *The Medical Language of St. Luke*. Dublin: Hodges, Figgis and Co., 1882.

Jaubert, A. *The Date of the Last Supper*. New York: Alba House, 1965. Translated from French.

Johnson, Luke Timothy. *The Acts of the Apostles*. Collegeville, Minnesota: The Liturgical Press, 1992.

Flavius, Josephus. *Antiquities of the Jews* — early history — William Whiston, translator. Edinburgh: William P. Nimmo Publishers, 1867. Standard version, Grand Rapids, Michigan: Kregel Publications, 1960.

Jung, Carl *Jung On Christianity*. Princeton: Princeton University Press, 1999.

Laughlin, J. C. H. "Capernaum From Jesus' Time and After," *Biblical Archaeology Review*, September/October, 1993.

Meier, John. *A Marginal Jew: Rethinking the Historical Jesus*, vol. 1. New York: Doubleday, 1991.

Miles, Jack. *Christ: A Crisis in the Life of God*. New York: Alfred A. Knopf, 2001.

Ogilvie, Lloyd J. *The Communicator's Commentary — Acts*. Waco: Word Books, 1983.

Pascal, Eugene. *Jung To Live By*. New York: Warner Books, Inc., 1992.

M. Scott Peck, *Golf And The Spirit*. New York: Harmony Books, 1999.

Peterman, Mary E. *Healing, A Spiritual Adventure*. Philadelphia: Fortress Press, 1974.

Quoist, Michael. *Prayers*. New York: Sheed and Werd, 1963.

Schonfield, H. J. *Those Incredible Christians, A New Look at the Early Church*. London: Hutchinson, 1968.

Schuller, Robert H. *Your Positive Plan for Love and Happiness*. New York: Inspirational Press, 1985, 1986.

Stevenson, Robert Louis. *A Child's Garden of Verses*. Edinburgh: Main Stream Publishing Company, 2001.

Walsh, J. *The Bones of St. Peter*. London: Victor Gollancz, 1983.

White, Anne S. *Healing Adventure*. Evesham, England, 1969.

Wilson, Ian. *Jesus: The Evidence — The Latest Research and Investigation*. San Francisco: HarperCollins, 2000.